D1468898

Thin Places

By Tim Bohlke

Thin Places

Copyright © 2018 by Tim Bohlke. Published by Harbor Ministries

ISBN: 0-9837843-1-0

I Won't Back Down.
Words and Music by Tom Petty and Jeff Lynne. Copyright (c) 1989 Gone Gator Music and EMI April Music Inc. All Rights for EMI April Music Inc., Administered by Sony/ATV Music Publishing LLC, 424 Church Street, Suite 1200, Nashbille, TN 37219. All Rights Reserved. Used by Permission. Reprinted by Permission of Hall Leonard LLC

Scriptures marked NIV are taken from the NEW INTERNATIONAL VERSION (NIV): Scripture taken from THE HOLY BIBLE, NEW INTERNATIONAL VERSION ®. Copyright© 1973, 1978, 1984, 2011 by Biblica, Inc.™. Used by permission of Zondervan

Scriptures marked CEV are taken from the CONTEMPORARY ENGLISH VERSION (CEV): Scripture taken from the CONTEMPORARY ENGLISH VERSION copyright© 1995 by the American Bible Society. Used by permission.

Scriptures marked NAS are taken from the NEW AMERICAN STANDARD (NAS): Scripture taken from the NEW AMERICAN STANDARD BIBLE®, copyright© 1960, 1962, 1963, 1968, 1971, 1972, 1973, 1975, 1977, 1995 by The Lockman Foundation. Used by permission.

Scriptures marked TM are taken from THE MESSAGE: THE BIBLE IN CONTEMPORARY ENGLISH (TM): Scripture taken from THE MESSAGE: THE BIBLE IN CONTEMPORARY ENGLISH, copyright©1993, 1994, 1995, 1996, 2000, 2001, 2002. Used by permission of NavPress Publishing Group

Harbor Ministries
PO Box 21984
Lincoln, NE 68542
info@harborministries.com

HarborMinistries.com

ON THE JOURNEY

DEDICATION

To my wife who is an over comer, a restorer, and a true warrior for the hearts of women. I am so honored to have you in my life.

To my kids, Drew, Ali and Dylan who have inspired me with their lives, resilience, courage, and passion for others and for life. With the season of life I am in, many of the stories in this book center around one of those kids, but they all have been the inspiration for so much of this work.

To the pastor who years ago told me that life and our spiritual journeys have a certain rhythm to them. He stated that our spiritual journeys are filled with questions, mystery, and adventure. He challenged me to go find it.

And finally, to the seven who journeyed to Iceland to simply chase a cliff. It was a memory of a lifetime and a moment none of us will ever forget.

PREFACE

This book is about moments. Moments when God shows up. Moments when God meets us. Moments when heaven and earth collide. The Celtic Christians called these moments thin places and I have adopted their language.

For the most part, this is my story. I am a dreamer, an adventurer, a cliff chaser. I experience God in the wild. I have come face to face with God on mountain tops, while sailing, in concert venues, even at Cowboy Church. But I also have been overwhelmed by his presence as I sat in my living room looking out at the snowy Nebraska landscape, or rode my bike on a trail near my home.

God can be in the grand experience. But mostly He is in the quiet, the ordinary, the day to day. In no way do I want to communicate that God only shows up in the extravagant or the extreme. God met Moses in an ordinary bush that Moses had likely passed by regularly in his work. *God met Moses at work!* He can meet you on a cliff in Iceland or on a quiet morning on your front porch. It's not about where God shows up, it's about our posture. Are we inclining our ears and souls toward God? When he nudges us, do we turn aside and look?

As you read this book my hope is that you will make space in life for thin places. That you will be ready for those everyday moments when God pulls back just a corner of the veil and reveals himself.

I am indebted to Mark Batterson, Ruth Haley Barton, and Thomas Cahill for their thinking and writing. Some of my thoughts were influenced by their books *Wild Goose Chase, Strengthening the Soul of Your Leadership,* and *How the Irish Saved Civilization.* I am also grateful to John Eldredge whose book *Wild at Heart* ignited my soul and set me on the journey of chasing cliffs.

THE CALL

It happened on a boardwalk in Mission Beach, California. I desperately needed to be alone, to have some space and find some peace. I wanted to hear something—anything—from God. The previous week had been the darkest our family had ever experienced. I felt like I had let them down; that somehow, I had failed to keep them safe. In the face of evil, I was angry, disappointed, and in some ways in shock. I was angry at God, and had lost heart. My faith journey was at a critical crossroads.

I didn't have the energy to do anything but sit. I hadn't been sleeping, waking frequently wondering if my family was safe. I'd never felt such a restless lack of peace. I'd never questioned with this kind of depth if I could really trust God. I wasn't sure what trust even meant anymore.

I had come to San Diego to plan for the next critical stage of a national ministry launch and I was totally numb. I wondered if I really had anything to offer the leaders who would soon arrive from around the country. What could I possibly tell them about this faith journey? Things were different now; I'd had enough. I was ready to walk away from this new ministry and even to walk away from God. I just wasn't sure I believed any of it any more. Anger and disappointment suffocated my soul. I was beyond hurting. I felt like I had literally been knocked out, and this time I wasn't sure I wanted to get up. It was impossible to see God in that moment—impossible to believe He was present at all. Plain and simple, it was a moment made for devastation.

I sat staring into the water, captivated by the swirling colors of the ocean. The sun was rising, and the waves seemed to bring the first moments of peace I'd felt in days. As I listened to my favorite Sigur Rós song, I sensed a deepening connection with all that was going on around me.

Then he approached. I didn't know him. My momentary peace was interrupted by what I can only describe as quiet rage as he approached. I didn't want to talk to him, but he ignored my nasty looks and clear disdain. With a quiet, compassionate, disarming look in his eyes, he signaled for me to take out my earphones.

"Have you ever been in such a peaceful place?" he asked.

"I don't know," I mumbled, "but it is pretty peaceful."

He pressed. "On a scale of one to five, where would you rate this place, this moment?"

"Maybe a two."

With great emotion, tears in his eyes, and strength in his voice he said, "I don't know what your top moments or places are, brother, but I'm totally overwhelmed by the peace of God at this moment. I hope you can be as well." Then he reached for my hand, and said, "God bless you, brother."

I was stunned, like I had been slapped in the face. I was suddenly in a very deep place. I stared at him for a moment, watched him interact with someone else, then turned my attention back to the ocean for not more than a few seconds, looked back and he was gone.

I had experienced a thin place.

A WILD MYSTERIOUS PURSUIT

The term "thin places" comes from this crazy group of radical Christians that has intrigued me for years. I have been captivated by their music, their customs, their close identity with nature, and their fiery faith that remained resilient through incredible circumstances.

The Celtic Christians came on the scene a few hundred years after the birth of Christ. The Roman Empire had fallen and spiritual darkness was overtaking Europe. In Ireland and northern England, a band of believers emerged who were anything but comfortable and safe in their faith. They were persecuted, warred against, and in an effort to eliminate them, pushed to outposts on the far edges of the North Sea.

Yet these enduring warriors of the faith not only survived, but thrived during one of the darkest spiritual times in human history. They were monks like St. Patrick who believed that God was not only wild and mysterious, but deeply personal and relational. They believed in a God who walks with us through all that life throws our way. They believed that no matter what, those moments with God are enough.

I could go on and on about why the Celtic Christians inspire me. They refused to forget or to become soft in their faith. They pursued God in extended times of solitude, fought for community, established and multiplied outpost monasteries in some of the most difficult geography and rugged terrain. They spread their influence throughout Europe, even to the far reaches of places like Iceland. These were not your ordinary monks we think of today. These were warrior monks fighting for the mission they were given—the preservation of scripture and culture.

I feel like I've been in some of those same spiritual battles. Since college I've struggled to not let my faith go soft, to not forget, to not let life with all its successes, failures, heartaches, and disappointments get in the way and block a clear pathway to God.

Did I mention that the Celtic Christians referred to God and the Holy Spirit as the Wild Goose?

THE WILD GOOSE

That name begs us to stop putting God in a box and begin to look at our spiritual journeys differently. It invites us to enter into this mysterious, different, and perhaps untamed nature of God that has remained undeniable throughout history. It serves notice that the Spirit of God cannot be tracked, boxed in, or controlled. I kind of like that. As Mark Batterson noted, it's a reminder that when it comes to God, there are elements of discovery, adventure, intrigue, and unpredictability that seem absent from our spiritual journeys today. Something about the idea of the Wild Goose is compelling. It calls us out. It forces us to embrace the mystery of God that too many of us have lost along the way. These radical Celtic Christians showed us a pathway to God that we desperately need.

I fear I've often tried to tame God. I confess to moments of wishing He was steady and predictable. Sometimes it would be nice to know what His next move was going to be. But the more I study and experience Him, the less I am sure of and the more I am drawn to the Wild Goose—to this mysterious, adventurous God and the unexpected ways He chooses to encounter us.

THIN PLACES

The Celtics called them "thin places." Those places and moments where heaven and earth collide, and just for a moment, the Wild Goose shows up and we experience life as it was meant to be. Those brief moments when the window cracks open and we get a fleeting glimpse into who God is. The kind of moments like I experienced on the boardwalk at Mission Beach.

If we pay attention, I believe God often calls out to us, reaches toward us, and invites us into these thin places. He inexplicitly shows up and makes

Himself known. He reminds us that He is real and that this spiritual pilgrimage has meaning and substance. It has a weightiness.

It is in these thin places God disrupts our lives. He shakes us out of our ruts and frees us of our expectations. He gives us what we need to take the next steps, strength to hang on when we need to hang on, and the wisdom and courage to let things go. In these thin places, our hearts ache for more.

This ache, this longing, this pursuit of the Wild Goose and thin places, took me and a band of brothers to Iceland, one of the landing places for those Celtic Christians as they expanded their scope and influence. We'd set out in search of an elusive cliff we'd seen in a music video. Now we were like the children following the drummer in that video; a drummer who perceived a rhythm that seemed just out of our reach.

THIS MAKES NO SENSE

To understand why we journeyed 3,400 miles to chase a cliff and the experience it represents, I need to tell you the story of how this group had been bound together for the past decade. It's a story that began in a thin place on a mountain overlooking Quito, Ecuador.

I was at the bottom. I crashed into midlife hard. I was depressed and struggling. I wanted out of the race. Looking back, it was similar to the way I would feel on Mission Beach years later. I was ready to give up on this whole spiritual journey. At a time when I felt most unworthy, most like I would not be able to finish this race, a man I had never met believed I had something important to say. Of all things, at a time when I was discouraged and in many ways ready to quit, he invited me to speak to weary youth leaders from around the world on what it takes to finish well. Only God does something like that.

It made no sense, but I got on that plane to South America trusting that God would show up. He would either show up and somehow use me to encourage those leaders to hang in there, stay the course, remember the key God moments in their lives, and to do what it takes to finish well, or it would be a case of awful timing or a sick cosmic joke. God did show up in a powerful way and He used that time to put some wind back in my sails. Strength started to return and I began to dream and journal again for the first time in months.

I got some time away and climbed a mountain outside the city. As I sat overlooking Quito, God awoke a dream—a literal dream He had given me years earlier. A clear vision began to emerge, and God whispered to me in a clear, compelling way. A phrase kept going through my mind, a rhythm that others could not yet hear.

You can change the world.

Tim, you can change the world, just twenty leaders at a time.

You need to invite people into something different, something intensely relational and deeply inspirational. You must remind leaders that no matter what life brings, no matter their successes or failures, they can know and experience God.

Then the vision became specific. This had to be something different. It needed to be a journey. Not a one-time shot, a flashy event, or a single inspirational moment. It must be a journey, a walk with God. Show leaders how to experience God for who He truly is—wild, mysterious, unpredictable. A fiercely loyal, relational God who won't withhold His love and affection forever.

Invite twenty leaders at a time into a three-year journey that could change the trajectory of their lives, their families, their businesses, and their ministries.

It made no sense, but I knew I had to do it. Or at least try.

A year later I invited two guys to Boulder, Colorado, to begin to think and dream about creating these life-changing experiences that could draw millennial leaders from around the country. As we were planning and dreaming, we saw a music video by Sigur Rós. I'll try to describe what we saw and some of the thoughts we had, but you should go to YouTube and watch the music video for "Glósóli" for yourself. Ben, who was with me in Boulder and one of the dreamers who joined me to launch this new ministry wrote these words about that video:

In the beginning, we find ourselves with a lone boy who carries nothing but a drum, tapping his foot in time with the subtle Kingdom rhythm he hears. The rhythm slowly takes hold and seems to transform his simple toe tapping into a desire to move, to go forth. The rhythm is constant, unchanging, and acts as the driving force for the journey that lies ahead.

As our lone drummer boy begins his trek across seemingly ravaged territory, he encounters children afraid to reveal themselves. The world is a dangerous place and offers little protection for these young ones. The first girl he meets is disguised as some form of wolf, having carefully crafted her defense from the predators of the wilderness. Our drummer simply beats his drum in time with the rhythm, and smiles as two other children come out of hiding, while the wolf girl begins to slowly reveal her true and beautiful face from behind her mask.

One lonely child has now become a small community journeying toward wherever it is this cadence may be taking them. They find more children, scattered and isolated, alone or in small groups. Their troupe of travelers continues to grow as they march across the desolate, yet beautiful landscape. No one is left behind as we see children offering kind, helpful hands to their companions as they cross difficult terrain. We find those who seek to love, begin to form relationships, hoping for their deepest and innermost fears to be met by another. On the lonely journey, they have found hope and healing in the connection of lives. Some of the children already seem to hear this Kingdom cadence, tapping their feet in time. Others are drawn by the passing travelers, inwardly beckoned to join the journey.

Along the way the band passes others intent on seeking their own forms of purpose, some through pointless destruction, others by equally pointless construction. Children burning things to the ground, and others building silly piles of rocks as high as they possibly can. As the drummer and his friends pass by, these children leave behind their building and destroying alike and follow. Our journeyers next come upon a sleeper, a dreamer perhaps. Instead of waking him from the quiet, they join him, finding their own rest and a sharing in his wonder.

The screen fades to black. The picture returns with a color tone reminiscent of a world of marvel. The rhythm they have been following begins to quicken... to beat more loudly... reverberating in their hearts... in their minds as they march up the gentle slope on the back side of the cliff. Finally, they reach the end of land, where they can walk no further. There they stand as one. Silent. Staring. Hoping. Dreaming of what it is that lies beyond the horizon. Our bold and brave drummer once again leads his followers with great courage *as he begins to loudly join the rhythm with the banging of his drum.*

Then, as though these young travelers are made for this moment, with a rebellious yell they break their stillness and charge toward the horizon. With the rogue courage to sprint as hard and fast as their small legs will take them, they begin to leave behind the unnecessary, for they will no longer need masks where they are journeying. They will no longer need a drum when they reach the source of all music. And as the end of the land approaches, they leap into the unknown. But instead of falling to their deaths they begin to take flight. Our initial dreamer is the most hesitant to jump. But this little doubter, inspired by the flight of others, makes the leap, and flies off after his fellow sojourners.

-Ben Harms

There we were. Grown men, seasoned, and well-traveled, and we felt like children. We could hear it. That slow steady beat that reverberates throughout all creation. The kingdom rhythm that beckoned us toward something greater than we could ever imagine. We knew what it was like to hide in a broken and desolate land, to wear masks, fearful of what danger lurks in the next corner. We had sought to find our meaning, our purpose, our substance in what we do. So we built things—often good, noble, and worthy things that have deep meaning and purpose, sometimes things that only built our own egos, our empires. We have destroyed things, even those things that we hold most dear to our hearts. We've created tall piles of rocks to prove something of ourselves. But our hearts beat for something more, something different.

I have no idea what Sigur Rós had in mind when they created this video, but as the story of the drummer boy in the "Glósóli" video unfolded, I felt like

I was watching the vision I had in Quito come to life. It made no sense. This Wild Goose had sent us affirmation and challenge through a music video created by an Icelandic post-rock band.

THE CLIFF

Nearly ten years later after that meeting in Colorado, I was in Iceland with my two sons and four co-conspirators who helped found Harbor Ministries. We journeyed to a remote part of the world in search of the cliff we'd seen in that video. We weren't even sure of its location. We knew it was somewhere on the Reykjanes Peninsula in the southwest part of Iceland, but that's a large area of roughly 320 square miles.

It was a Wild Goose chase.

Each morning, as we awoke in a remote house in Iceland, we talked. We shared stories of the amazing things God had done since we'd first set out to create Harbor Ministries. God showed up in those stories, in the emotion and the passion we shared as we talked about life after life that had been transformed. As we named leader after leader who had entered Harbor desperate for hope and emerged believing they could meet God in a transforming way, we found ourselves in a thin place.

More of these thin places—these moments outside time and beyond our comprehension—happened as we shared lava stew at the base of a recently active volcano, and ate fish and chips at one of the oldest fishing villages in Iceland. We found thin places as we walked behind towering waterfalls during a midnight sunset. It seemed that around every corner we caught glimpses of the Wild Goose. Our journey was, in part, rebellion. We were fighting back the urge to merely coast through the next seasons of our lives. We were rebelling against the pressure to settle in and go peacefully into the sunset. Our hearts screamed for more, so we journeyed to this land of fire and ice.

Iceland is one of the few places in the world where the continental drift has caused two continents to collide and push a land mass above ocean level. As I walked down to the thin canyon and reached one arm toward Europe and the other toward North America, I found myself in a thin place that demanded my attention. Just like you can stand at the Four Corners Monument and be in four different states at once, so in Iceland you can reach toward two continents. Surely a God who orchestrates the drift of continents is someone that I can trust. As I stood there with one foot in Europe and the other in North America, I felt incredibly small, and God was, well, much, much bigger.

It's a land of wild beauty. Rock cliffs go straight up to the sky, black beaches line the coasts, and countless towering waterfalls cascade over volcanic rock. It's a place where it's hard to deny the existence of a divine creator, a place where my soul resonated with the words of Psalm 42:7, "Deep calls to deep in the roar of your waterfalls; all your waves and breakers have swept over me."

HISTORIC PURSUITS

Throughout scripture, we see God invite people into thin places, and what happens in those thin places disrupts the world. Abraham gives up everything based on a promise he received in the night. Moses, likely content to live out his life in the desert running his father-in-law's business, runs into God in a thin place. His life, his family, and history are altered. A young David takes on a giant, and a whole nation rallies and routes an enemy. After spending time with God, Gideon radically follows God's leading and reduces his army from around 30,000 to 300 and takes on a far superior enemy.

There are the hundreds of thin place encounters Jesus has with people throughout the gospels. There is this moment when He reaches out to brothers James and John and invites them to follow him. Their response is so immediate that the text in Mark says they left their father in the boat to follow Jesus. In another moment, a rich young ruler approaches Jesus and asks what he must do to have eternal life. Jesus says, "Sell everything, give it all away and follow me." Or there was a simple moment when a woman reaches out to just touch the hem of Jesus' robe and he turns to her and says, "Your faith has made you whole."

Or there was Paul. Paul made it his mission to round up, persecute and kill those who followed Jesus. He rode into the desert in hot pursuit of more Christians to kill, but instead had a thin place encounter with God that was so intense he was knocked off his mule and blinded. And then everything changed.

And Peter. Peter was carrying on the family business, and though he may not have been catching many fish at the time, it was a living. It was what he needed to do to survive. But here came this man who joined him on his boat, encouraged him, then invited him to leave everything and join him on an adventure—an adventure filled with incredible and heartbreaking moments, inspiration, and struggle. To say Jesus disrupted Peter's life would be a mild understatement.

When you read that story, do you wonder why Peter left everything to follow someone into the total unknown? At the same time, if you're honest, do you understand Peter? Is something in you aching for that kind of interruption? Do you long to be invited into a much bigger and more compelling story?

I did.

That's how I found myself in Iceland.

A LIFE-SAVING ENCOUNTER

I opened this book describing a moment on Mission Beach when God pulled back the veil. Somehow, in the middle of all that I was going through, there was this messenger—someone who, in a matter of a few seconds, provided a moment of peace in the storm. A messenger who went right to my wound. In that moment, the intense anger and hurt that was beginning to consume me lost its grip on me.

That thin place kept me in this faith journey. It kept me engaged enough to continue down the road of launching a national ministry. Yet, in the days after that encounter I still wondered why God seems to show up so unassuming, so subtly yet so powerfully at times, and at other times seems so quiet, so absent, so uninvolved, so detached. I still wondered if He is with us. Is He really there in the darkest, most horrific moments of life? And if He is, why doesn't He do something about it? Why doesn't He intervene to stop the pain? I didn't have answers, but for the first time in a while I had hope. I didn't understand it, but I knew that for a brief moment with an ocean, a song, and a stranger, I had an encounter with the Creator and it left me longing for more.

But I knew I had to keep moving toward Him. If that moment at Mission Beach was a glimpse of what was to come, I simply had to continue the pursuit, because if someday, somehow, we are able to live in those kind of moments... this faith journey would be so worth the fight. That is what I needed to tell those pastors and leaders who would gather in San Diego: No matter what life throws at us, success, failure, bitter disappointment, struggle, tragedy, or epic moments, God walks through all of it with us. In the darkest places and the brightest moments, He walks with us.

SPACE FOR DISRUPTION

I have heard others talk about these thin place moments when heaven and earth collide. One day my mom was driving home after running some errands. We lived in the country so running errands meant a long drive into town. As she drove, she felt a strong sense that she was to drive another twenty miles to visit a woman who'd recently joined a small group she was a part of. She heeded that holy nudge. When she arrived, she found the woman just moments from taking her own life.

My mom was a bit of a mystic. This idea of thin places would not be new to her. She experienced many moments when she not only sensed direction, but she acted on it. She was alert to God's promptings. She made space for the interruptions.

Finding space for God to get our attention is a struggle for many of the leaders who come to Harbor. Chad is a successful businessman in Nashville. He came into a recent Rhythm in Twenty leadership journey on fumes, tired, and a little disillusioned in his faith. I could tell by the look on his face he was desperate to encounter God in a tangible way. He came with a major project deadline looming and a lot of work on his plate. But after the first night he realized he needed to call his client and tell him the project needed to wait, because he needed to be fully present in the Rhythm experience during those four days in Colorado. As Chad began to quiet down and listen, things began to happen. He sent me this message in a text a few months after our time in Colorado:

"Thanks for following your dream of investing in just twenty leaders at a time. I know from our first time together that I will never be the same. I'll never lead the same. I'll never be the same husband, father, friend, brother, boss, or child of God."

And he is not alone. Over and over and over again we hear from leaders who have encountered God in the space that Harbor helps them create.

"Thanks for the mission of Harbor, thanks for stepping out and taking a chance. You have not dropped a pebble in the pond, you have dropped a hellfire missile in it. And the waves will beat the shores of time for generations to come" -Jon

"This journey has been the most transformational two years of my life. By slowing down, carving out time and listening, things have changed. I was not sure if I could finish this race, I almost gave up, but learning to live with a different rhythm, has given me renewed vision and breathed fresh wind into my lungs." -Tom

Change happens when we make space for God to create thin places.

I have seen that hunger, that hope, that almost desperate look. It's in the eyes of leaders from all over the country who have come to Colorado to embark on one of our leadership journeys. It's as if they're saying, "Tell me this is real. I need to know that this faith journey I'm giving my life to is worth it. Tell me that God really does show up, that I can experience Him even in the midst of the fast pace and crushing busyness."

And we tell them and show them that, yes, we can see and experience God if we just slow down enough to listen, to watch, and to be alert to those moments when the window cracks open. That's when we see God and get a glimpse of life as it was intended to be.

I need thin places. I need to experience God. A two-minute encounter on Mission Beach changed everything for me. Heaven and earth collided, and for a moment God broke through the dense fog, confusion, and intensity of life. I caught just a glimpse in that thin place, but it was enough. Things changed. A moment of peace returned. I know that this spiritual journey is real. The questions and struggles did not go away, but the way I would walk through them changed.

That moment was a picture of what the pursuit of the cliff in Iceland was all about. That moment helped define the why of Harbor Ministries. It clarified why I would continue to give my life to this mission. It helped answer the question of why I must stay on this faith journey myself. It became the why for eight sojourners on this crazy trip to Iceland.

The cliff became a visual reminder that somehow through the gray, the fog, the darkness, there are moments we can see God. While the journey may be desolate and lonely, the obstacles and the struggles great, the distractions many, the pressure to coast and settle intense, and the ongoing questions immense, we still need to chase that cliff. We need to seek it out, find it, climb it, and be willing to take the leap of faith. We need that hope. We need to know that the pursuit of God brings adventure, risk, and mystery.

That's the invitation. It is the essence of who the Wild Goose is and of what He calls us to.

Let's find that cliff.

PART ONE THE WHY

THE PERFECT STORM

In 1991, six men aboard the fishing vessel Andrea Gail sailed into the perfect storm. They left Gloucester Harbor, Massachusetts, headed toward Newfoundland. The fishing was poor so Captain Billy Tyne took the vessel further out to sea. As they headed for home, the Andrea Gail sailed right into what was later termed the perfect storm. A hurricane was heading up the Northeast coast from the Gulf of Mexico, and a Nor'easter was rolling through Canada and out to sea off the New England coast. The two storms were about to collide. No one could anticipate the chaos and danger that would follow.

Several years ago, I was executive director of a large Youth for Christ chapter in the Midwest. This organization grew from three salaried employees to forty-five employees who reached thousands of teenagers every week. In many ways, it was the best of times. We had a dynamic and growing ministry team, we effectively impacted not just a handful of students, but entire high school and middle school campuses. Other leaders came our way to see how it was done.

But cracks were developing under the surface. No one knew. I wasn't even aware. A perfect storm was brewing in my life and leadership journey. Boredom, fatigue, and disappointment roiled and were about to converge. These are the kind of things that take leaders out. Left unchecked, a perfect storm can devastate lives, families, careers, and ministries. I wish I had been more alert and recognized what I now see so clearly.

BOREDOM. I had been with Youth for Christ for more than twenty years. I felt like I could do some aspects of my job with my eyes closed. But it wasn't just work. I was bored in relationships, in marriage, in life. I was just flat out bored.

FATIGUE. I was responsible not only for a team of young staff, but also for the funds that made this whole thing go. Year after year I was raising hundreds of thousands of dollars. I seldom shared the weight of that burden with others, or asked others to help me carry that responsibility. In many ways, I was on a lonely journey and it was wearing on me.

DISAPPOINTMENT. I was disappointed in myself, in others, in some of my life circumstances. And to be honest, I was disappointed in God. This disappointment was starting to shape my view of the world and influence my decision-making.

So there I was, the leader of a large ministry. Who could I talk to about these things? Who could I tell? Who could I really be honest with and say, "Hey, I'm in trouble here. I'm afraid I'm going to make some reckless decisions out of sheer boredom. I may be done with this job. I'm feeling like it's time to move on. But is that okay? Is it okay to move on? And how do I tell all these people that I have recruited into this organization?" I felt like I had built this large organization, but along the way I had given up some of the things I am most passionate about. Somehow I had lost some of myself along the way.

That is one of the great complexities of leadership. Whom do you talk to when you're struggling, questioning, wavering? The board? Staff? Donors whom you've built relationships with? Your family who is depending on your consistence and stability? The truth is, I had failed. I had failed to build a group of allies, trusted people, and truth-tellers who would help me think things through.

So this perfect storm continued to form and I came dangerously close to making costly decisions that could have wreaked havoc on my life.

After a year of being pursued by a large church to join their senior leadership team, and despite years of saying I would never work at a church, I decided to take the job. In part, I thought that if I changed things up maybe I could quiet the restless stir that was still growing.

Six months into that journey I had an emotional crash. I was in the eye of the storm.

I recount this story of my own perfect storm because I don't think it's rare—especially for those on the front lines of leading ministries, organizations, and businesses that are seeking to transform the world. I share this story because I've seen the devastation these storms leave in their wake. The broken marriages.

The burned-out leaders. The moral failures. The hollow shells of numb leaders who were once dangerous to the enemy. The disillusioned followers and donors. The sullied named of Christ.

And I want it to end. I want to find ways for leaders to meet God in those thin places. I want God to disrupt the storm and to shake us free of our malaise. But first, we must learn to recognize the indicators that we're in danger.

BOREDOM

During an incredible day of discovery in Iceland, we took this side road off Highway 36 on the way to Vik. There was something compelling about the scene before us: a beautiful glacier-fed waterfall and the little church off in the distance. The clouds were thick and gray and rain was increasing. We opened the horse gate on the muddy dirt road and drove into the small village. We were drawn toward the quaint church that had been founded centuries earlier.

I sat in one of the pews and tried to imagine being a priest or monk, likely with Celtic roots and passion, feeling the call to Iceland in the 1500s. I mean, what would that have been like to be called to a place of frigid temperatures and barren landscapes, with only a small rock house for shelter?

We approached the pulpit where a Bible laid open. It was dated 1586. So more than 400 years ago, someone felt so compelled by the people of Iceland that they crossed the icy North Sea from Europe and settled in. And for a time, this church, and Christianity in general, flourished in this place. Standing in that church I could feel the raw, wild, incredible faith of these early Celtic Christians.

Yet there we stood, hundreds of years later and the church, although well kept, stood mostly empty. It had clearly lost its way, as Christianity has in much of Iceland. Locals shared with us that the church had lost its relevance, and faith in God seemed to have no compelling purpose to the people there. How could this have happened? The early priests and Christians had endured so much, but those fierce warriors of the faith are seemingly gone.

What happened there? Was it a brutal full-on assault? Was the church outlawed and forced underground? Or was it something much subtler but just as deadly that took hold of people, flattening their spiritual journeys and wreaking havoc on their faith? No doubt disappointment, fatigue, and deep spiritual boredom settled in, leaving behind that hallow church as a reminder of the vibrant life that was once there.

Standing outside that church that day was such a powerfully empty moment. It was sad. It reminds me of what is happening in America today, a slow but steady fade, a spiritual darkness that seems to be spreading. I had been in a church that reminded me of this one. The building was newer, but the spiritual temperature was the same. Cold. Lifeless.

My son Dylan was attending basketball camp in North Carolina. It was a dream trip for him. He got to play in front of Roy Williams, and a future NBA player was the referee for his first game. For a thirteen-year-old, it was as good as it gets. While in Chapel Hill, I popped in on a service in a little Methodist church on the edge of campus. The message that day was a great reminder of living with mission and pursing the dreams that God had given us.

The pastor described ministry as, "The work of God, done together by the people of God utilizing their gifts, strengths, and dreams. God works through the dreams of his people who long to reach and serve the culture, the hurting, and the searching. Ministry is accomplished when we love others and come alongside them. Ministry is accomplished when we stay true to our mission."

He asked us to look around the building, to see its beauty, but to remember why it was built on the North Carolina campus; it was built to reach and impact the future leaders on that campus. What was so striking about that moment for me was that as I looked around, there was a total of about four college-age people in the whole place, maybe two families, and the rest were all very old. Somewhere along the way, this strategically located church that was founded with great vision and mission, had completely lost its way. It had forgotten its mission, and even though the guy was preaching a good word, I had to wonder if somehow along the way he'd lost his edge.

I believe one of the biggest problems among Christians in America today is boredom. So many of us lack a compelling vision, a challenge, an adventure. We ache to be called into something greater than ourselves. We long to have a significant, difference-making role in the mission. Let's face it, so often church and religion in and of itself can feel boring and lifeless. But pursuing and being pursued by a wild, unpredictable, sometimes random, mysterious God? That's not boring. That's compelling!

Whether in the church, in our relationships, or in our vocations, when boredom settles in, we lose interest. We look in other places, our eyes, minds, and hearts start to wander, and we look for things that will fill that gap and create adventure. Sometimes those things can have a positive impact and be just plain fun. It was in seasons of boredom that I learned the banjo, found a passion for mountain biking, took some of my best trips, and experienced some amazing adventures. But if we let ourselves get stuck in those seasons of boredom, we can start to coast and begin to settle. It becomes easier and easier to fill the gaps in our lives with some destructive stuff.

Recently our church has been studying 1 and 2 Samuel and the life of King David. Throughout these books, you see a storm forming in David's life. While there was a specific moment when his life and leadership took a dark turn, there was likely a long decline going on in his spiritual journey that got him to that place. I can't help but wonder what role disappointment, fatigue, and boredom played in that decline. How did it tempt him to settle for less in his relationship with God? David's subtle slide, his loss of a passionate pursuit of God had devastating results.

David's story is incredible! You can't make this stuff up. He went from shepherd boy to giant killer, to hero and hope of an entire nation. Then he was a falsely accused fugitive constantly on the run from a corrupt and flawed king. Finally, David emerged to his true calling as king—a king who was welcomed and celebrated. Many gladly died for King David because they knew that he was a man after God's own heart; a man, and now a king, who inspired with his actions, his heart, his bravery, and his all-out pursuit of God. Under his God-honoring reign, the Nation of Israel flourished and defeated many of its enemies.

When we pick up the story many years later, the years seem to have taken a toll. We see a tired and likely very bored leader who had settled in. All of his success clearly took his journey in the wrong direction. After years of military victories, wealth, and unmatched privilege, this king was coasting. He had become entitled. Now his army was off at war and he had stayed behind. The brave warrior and military leader was now apparently content to let others fight those battles. So we find King David on the roof of his palace, pacing. Looking. Waiting. Wondering. Then something caught his eye. A beautiful woman bathing on the roof just one house over. While that moment might make any man vulnerable, a bored man with a sense of entitlement was in big trouble.

The king who once leaned into his calling, a leader who stepped out in faith against incredible odds because he knew God would be with him, was now in a very dangerous place. In his boredom, he was about to invite the kind of adventure into his life that would ultimately destroy his family, cost many lives, and nearly destroy his ability to lead a country.

How did he get here? David had a deep, personal, engaging relationship with God. We see a picture of this in 2 Samuel 5:19 (ESV), "Then David inquired of the Lord, 'Shall I go up against the Philistines? Will you give them into my hand?' And the Lord said to David, 'Go up for I will certainly give the Philistines into your hand'... the Lord has broken through my enemies before me like the breakthrough of waters."

Yes, David was a man after Gods own heart, and yes, God did go before him in battle, time and time again. This was a focused, humble leader who chased after God with the kind of passion that made him dangerous to any enemy who wanted to get in his way or take him out. This warrior king entered the city gates of Jerusalem leaping and dancing for joy before God. He humbly offered burnt and peace offerings in the name of the Lord. Nathan, God's prophet, affirmed David's role as king of Israel.

But, in the years that followed, his perfect storm was forming, and a much different story would begin to be told—the tragic turn in David's leadership would begin in a single moment on that roof top. Unfortunately, this is a common theme in the stories of too many leaders. Often, it's not the struggles or the hard times that derail leaders, but times of extended prosperity, success, coasting, and safety that can take us out spiritually.

Biking is one of my passions. Often just a forty-minute ride on a stressful day is a great escape. Biking has also given me some insights on life. If you've ever watched the Tour de France, you know that most of the crashes happen on the down hills when the bikers are coasting. So it was with David.

In David's case, battle after battle had been won. Victory became common place. The most powerful armies of the day were defeated. The seasons continued to change and the years piled up one after the other. "Then it happened in the spring, at the time when kings go out to battle, that David sent Joab and his servants with him and all of Israel... But David stayed at Jerusalem... Now when evening came David arose from his bed..." 2 Samuel 11:1-2 (NASB).

Did you catch that? It says, "When evening came, David arose from his bed." That sounds like a tired, bored leader to me, not getting out of bed until evening. David was headed for certain trouble because when a man steps back from what he was called to be, when he begins to sit back and let others fight his battles, when he sleeps in and has idle time, when he becomes so bored he looks for something to give him an adrenaline rush. That's when so many stories take a tough turn.

"David arose from his bed and walked around on the roof of the king's house, and from the roof he saw a woman bathing, and the woman was very beautiful in appearance." 2 Samuel 11:2 (NASB).

So David was walking around on the roof with nothing to do. He was probably wondering if he should have gone to battle after all. He slept the day away, now he paced and the moment presented itself. And like so many of us who come up against these kinds of moments, David failed to consider the future consequences. He was king after all. What could possibly happen? There was nothing he couldn't manipulate or control.

"So David sent messengers and took her, and when she came to him he lay with her." 2 Samuel 11:4 (NASB).

What unfolds from that point on was lying, cover ups, and murder. It most likely wasn't just Bathsheba's husband that David sent to the front lines to be killed. It was likely Uriah and his entire company that were sent to the front lines. You could say that it was not just a murder, but an act of mass murder, and it all started with a king sleeping the day away then pacing on his roof on a hot night.

The fatigue, the compromise, the boredom that led to that evening when David slept with Bathsheba changed the trajectory of his reign. From that point forward, that warrior king, that boy who defeated a giant, shrunk back and became small. He became passive, fearful to lead, and hesitant to take a stand. Even more tragic, he seemingly lost that powerful, personal, conversational connection to God.

Boredom set in for me as I was finishing my second decade with Youth for Christ. The compelling mission of that organization was fading for me. Through those years of work at Youth for Christ, there were a few things that I could always count on. There was often stress around fundraising. Early on I always wondered if I had raised enough money to get paid that month. Later the stakes were higher and I pondered if enough resources had come in to keep the large staff and organization running well. If you read my journals from the last several years of my time there, you would find the same questions every spring.

Can I do this again? Can I start another intense ministry year? Am I ready to sign up for another round? I'm tired of the routine. I'm bored and dying for a new challenge.

And I can imagine David asking the same kinds of questions.

Can I do this again? Can I start another intense round of battles? Am I ready to march out again? I'm sick of the routine.

And as the years went on, my questions and the struggles described in my journals expanded.

I am so ready for something different. I can do this with my eyes closed. I am bored. Is this all there is going to be for me? This is not where I thought I would be. I am tired of tight finances, constant fundraising, and the pressure of helping provide for so many people and their families.

I could never fully name it until a few years ago, but the truth is, it was boredom. I was bored stiff. I was bored with the mundane, the repetitiveness, and the routine needed to run a successful large organization. My boredom extended well beyond work. I was totally bored at church. I was bored in my marriage. I was bored in my spiritual journey. I thought many times that if this was all that faith in God was about—doing, working, praying, checking the boxes and experiencing what seemed like so much silence—if that was it, then I wanted out. I had lost my edge, and the faith journey was just not compelling enough anymore. The weight of leading, encouraging and inspiring others was taking a toll. In the busyness and years of "doing" all this work for God, I had somewhere, somehow lost that personal connection. I was not meeting and encountering God in deeply personal ways anymore, so how could I effectively lead others down that path? The truth was, I was trying to take people to places that I was no longer going myself. I had lost my way.

I have been compelled by Moses as a leader for years. He spent forty years as a shepherd doing the same thing every day. Then in a razor thin moment, in the middle of the day-to-day grind, God broke through. After forty years of virtual isolation, God chose him to lead the Israelites out of bondage. Moses himself doubted that he was the man for the job. Who was he that a whole nation of people would follow him? He was not a gifted motivational speaker. He grew up in the privileged life of Pharaoh's household where not much was asked or demanded of him. Then he spent four decades with sheep. It's not hard to imagine why he struggled with the incredible mission God had given him. Why would a nation of hundreds of thousands follow him?

Plain and simple, people would follow Moses because he met with God. They would see it in his face, they'd know it by his actions, and see it in the results. Throughout the exodus and then the exile in the wilderness, God often met Moses in thin places. When Moses needed to hear from God, he would wait. He waited forty years in the desert. He waited forty days on Mount Siani. At one point when he needed to desperately hear from God, he waited in his tent until God showed up. Moses made it a regular proactive practice to pursue those thin moments with God, and the people followed him because of it. I knew those personal encounters with Him were what was missing in my life and leadership and it was time to get them back.

In her book *Strengthening the Soul of Your Leadership*, Ruth Haley Barton writes "Only a leader that has waited for God in their darkest moments of his own deep need, only a leader who has stood still and waited for God's deliverance in the places where she feared for her very life, only the leader with inner spiritual authority that comes from his own waiting, can ask others to do the same."

I had stopped waiting.

Through all the years of ministry, leadership, and service, I started to miss the practice of breaking away for those longer times of quieting down, listening, and seeking God. I had neglected extended times of quiet and solitude. As a result, I had lost the spark, the passion, the edge I so needed to do this journey well. In many ways I was still able to go through the motions. I still worked hard. I still loved my family and enjoyed being a dad. But that passionate pursuit of God that made me dangerous had slipped. I was used to success. I took fewer risks. I played it safe.

I was at the edge of making decisions that could have cost me greatly. Yet God met me on that mountain overlooking Quito, Ecuador. In that tired, beaten down, and bored place, God awakened a dream that had come many years earlier. He reignited a mission that re-engaged my heart. New passions stirred. He shook me out of my malaise and gave me a calling so big I didn't have time to be bored.

One of my favorite stories in the Bible is about two guys who fought against boredom and safety. They took a huge risk and stepped out to face a superior enemy and, as a result, rallied an entire army.

Jonathan could have given into boredom. God asked him to wait in a holding pattern for a long time. He was disappointed, frustrated, and tired of sitting around while his father, King Saul, refused to act. As the powerful Philistine army built up its forces of men, chariots, armor, and weapons, Saul was immobilized by doubt, fear, indifference, questions about his own leadership, and a sense that God was no longer with him. His army was holed up in caves waiting for what would be certain defeat. They hid, many of them content to wait it out and not fight. And part of them must have been bored stiff.

Finally, Jonathan had enough. He had enough sitting, waiting, and hiding. He had enough of watching his dad sit on his ass and do nothing. So he talked to the young man who carried his armor and developed a plan for the two of them to approach the strongest position of the enemy.

Now the day came that Jonathan, the son of Saul, said to the young man who was carrying his armor, 'Come and let us cross over to the Philistines' garrison that is on the other side.' But he did not tell his father... 'Come and let us cross over to the garrison of these uncircumcised; perhaps the Lord will work for us, for the Lord is not restrained to save by many or by few.' His armor bearer said to him, 'Do all that is in your heart; turn yourself, and here I am with you according to your desire.' Then Jonathan said, 'Behold, we will cross over to the men and reveal ourselves to them. If they say to us, 'Wait until we come to you'; then we will stand in our place and not go up to them. But if they say, 'Come up to us,' then we will go up, for the Lord has given them into our hands; and this shall be the sign to us.' When both of them revealed themselves to the garrison of the Philistines, the Philistines said, 'Behold, Hebrews are coming out of the holes where they have hidden themselves.' So the men of the garrison hailed Jonathan and his armor bearer and said, 'Come up to us and we will tell you something.' And Jonathan said to his armor bearer, 'Come up after me, for the Lord has given them into the hands of Israel.'
1 Samuel 14:1-12 (NASB)

This is one of the great moments in the Bible. And the best part is the six words in verse four where Jonathan says, "Hey, let's go do this impossible, crazy thing, and perhaps God will be with us." Think about that. They were tired, bored, frustrated and unwilling to wait any longer. So Jonathan unpacked this wild plan with no guarantees, no assurance of safety. In fact, if God didn't show up, they were dead. It's counter intuitive, right? We want assurances. We build so much of our lives around this idea of safety. We try to keep our kids safe, keep them back from the edge, discourage them from taking too many risks. No wonder we live in a society where boredom is becoming epidemic.

What if the most risky and dangerous thing is not coming too close to the edge, but staying back where it is safe... staying in that place where things are known and more secure...

We have had some great family adventures over the years, but one of our favorites was a long road trip through Utah and Arizona several years ago. There were stops to see some awesome national parks, incredible hikes, and some jet skiing on Lake Powell. (An absolute must if you have not been there!) But maybe the top spot was getting to the north rim of the Grand Canyon at sunset and taking a mule ride down into the canyon the next morning. One of the things I remember was how much time we spent reminding our kids to stay back from the edge of the canyon, to not get too close. With a risk-taking twelve-year-old who often walked to the beat of his own drum,we were never all that comfortable. Our understandable instincts were to protect and insulate our kids from risk; to keep them safe.

Now I wonder if these messages of safety, of pulling back, of not getting too close we heard as children, have stuck with us as adults, especially in our spiritual journeys. I wonder if pulling back from the edge keeps us from experiencing the kind of life we were meant to live. What if the edge is actually the place we need to go? What if there is opportunity, adventure, risk, needed perspective, and life-giving mission and necessary vision that can only be seen from that vantage point?

What if it is actually more risky to settle in, stay safe, stay back in the places where we are familiar and comfortable? What if the most dangerous choice is actually staying a few feet back, settling in and allowing our view to be hindered?

Let's pay attention to Jonathan and his young servant. What can we learn about not just playing it safe but breaking out of boredom? Maybe there is something in their story that will make sense to you in your journey.

THIS IS A STORY POWERED BY RELATIONSHIP

Through experience, adventure, success, and failure, a deep relationship formed between Jonathan and his armor bearer centered on courage and trust. They challenged each other and had each other's backs. A great part of this story comes in the words of the young arms bearer. As Jonathan lays out his crazy plan, the arms bearer basically says, "Do what is on your heart, I am with you no matter what." That kind of communication and connection around a common mission is something we all want and hope for.

THEY WERE CONVINCED A MUCH BIGGER STORY WAS PLAYING OUT

Jonathan realized there was something much bigger than the battle that they were bogged down in, and much bigger than the story of hiding and fear they were currently living. It was bigger even than their own lives, and they were convinced they had a role in it.

THERE IS A TIME FOR COURAGE

There are times when God calls us to step out, maybe even to go beyond logic and reason. At times God asks us to go against impossible odds with no guarantees other than believing that if God shows up, anything can happen.

AGAINST OBSTACLES AND UNCERTAINTY, THEY DID NOT LOSE HEART

The battles had not diminished their faith. In fact, they had strengthened their faith. And what happened because of their actions?

> When all the men of Israel who had hidden themselves in the hill country of Ephraim heard that the Philistines had fled, even they also pursued them closely in the battle. So the Lord delivered Israel that day...
> 1 Samuel 14:22-23 (NASB)

Because of the action of two men, an entire army was infused with courage, and an incredible battle against overwhelming odds was won that day. This story shows us that amazing things can happen through the lives of tired, disillusioned, disappointed, and bored men and women, who are determined not to get stuck or to settle.

It's time for some self-assessment. Has boredom set in in some area of your life? If so, it helps to name it. Write the word "BORED" in your journal then do some thinking and processing around that word. Is there anything in your work, relationships, or personal world you need to think about regarding this word? Is there any place where boredom has taken hold and begun to choke out your passion? Rigidness, boredom, unnecessary structure, and routine are just a few of the things that kill passion and cause us to lose heart.

The 1985 movie "The Breakfast Club" centers on several kids from diverse backgrounds who are stuck in the library for a long day of detention. The entire movie takes place in that one day. As the kids begin to find common ground, they talk about their parents. One of them notes that their parents have stopped having fun and are just going through the motions of life. In fact, one of the kids says, "My parents have just lost heart." The parents have given up and it's impacted their kids! Let that sink in. I know I don't want to get stuck in a routine, get bored, and lose heart. I want to do my best to keep an edge to my life for as long as I have.

Ask yourself if you are stuck in a lifeless spiritual routine. If so, what are you personally willing to do about it? It could be as simple as shaking things up. Drive a different way home, have that extra conversation, reach out to someone you have been thinking about, take a risk, or when you would typically move to the next thing, rush to work or rush home... linger for a moment. Spontaneously pull over. Stop. Wait. Listen.

Is there a step of courage you could take in your relationships, your work, or your personal spiritual journey? Maybe it's time to act on something that has been on your mind for a long time? Is there a "perhaps God..." thin place moment waiting for you? Is there a step you need to take to light a fire and engage yourself and others in a more passionate pursuit of this wild mysterious God? Is there an adventure that you need to plan, or a cliff you need to chase?

That is part of what makes Harbor Ministries and the Rhythm in Twenty and Rogue events so unique. We invite leaders to step out of their comfort zones, take a chance, embrace an adventure, and enter into a raw and vulnerable pursuit of God again.

Do not let boredom lead to devastating decisions. Re-engage your soul before you find yourself pacing on a roof top.

FATIGUE

One thing that was powerful and sometimes overwhelming about exploring Iceland is that we were very aware we were in a very active, living, constantly changing environment. The indicators are everywhere: Fire, ice, steam from geothermal activity, hot springs, glacier melt waterfalls, and volcanic ash from recent eruptions all within short drives of each other. There are more volcanic eruptions in Iceland than any other place in the world. In 2010, several eruptions of Eyjafjallajökull grounded flights in Europe for six days and continued to disrupt air travel for weeks. We walked across the volcanic ash and the black sand beaches left from the fallout. The destruction and power of those eruptions had to have been intense, but what we saw and experienced years later was beautiful, captivating, and inviting.

Scientists are constantly taking measurements and watching the Icelandic landscape for indicators of the next big eruption. Signs of impending eruption are often very subtle or too well hidden to make predicting volcanic events an exact science. Still, teams of scientists devote themselves to studying, watching, and listening for whatever warning signs may show themselves.

A few years ago, I checked a major item off my bucket list—fly fishing with my sons in Montana. It was incredible! We were on the Yellowstone River fishing with double flies. The guide coached us as we floated this fast river and taught us that a dry fly on top of the water was the key to catching fish. With the rush of the river, the action of the boat, the thrill of one of us landing a cutthroat or rainbow trout, and the incredible natural beauty all around us, it was so easy to take our eyes off the indicator and miss what was happening under the surface. Unless you were attending to the dry fly—I mean paying close attention, focused, watching, and waiting for that subtle hit on the line—you were going to miss some adrenaline-filled excitement. We caught some amazing trout that day, but I can't tell you how many fish I missed because of the distractions around me. Don't get me wrong. Soaking in some of the sights was sometimes worth it, but losing focus, getting distracted, and missing the signs of the indicator caused us to miss many, many fish.

This idea of indicators has become a major theme for me, particularly as I've thought about fatigue. I have missed so many indicators in my life, and at one point, it led to the perfect storm I described earlier.

When I was leading Youth for Christ a ton of affirmation was coming my way, but below the surface, some cracks were beginning to show. Loneliness, boredom, and this restless stir was setting in. I was so distracted and those around me were so busy that we missed the signs—the indicators—that spiritual, emotional, and some physical fatigue was taking hold. I was so busy, and so preoccupied with the urgent, that I had lost sight of the passion around the mission that got me into this in the first place. I had lost sight of the dry fly.

As the fatigue around fundraising, leading a large staff and hundreds of volunteers, and the added stress of a building project continued to take a toll, the indicators continued to reveal themselves. I was underestimating their significance, or missing them altogether. And my situation was not unique. This dynamic is too prevalent in our leadership culture. I've seen it in the lives of the ministry and business leaders who arrive at Harbor events spiritually, emotionally, and physically fatigued.

We see it in the life of Moses. He hit the wall big time and it took the intervention of a father-in-law, among others, to get him back on track. That part of the story is told in Exodus 18:14-26. See if you can relate.

Moses was running hard and fast. Too often he alone was the leader, the decision maker, the judge, and the jury for the nation of Israel. He said as much in verses 15-16 (NASB), "Because the people come to me to seek God's will, whenever they have a dispute, it is brought to me... and I inform them of God's decrees and instructions."

It's true that Moses was the go to between God and the people, but he had positioned himself in an absolutely unsustainable situation and his father-in-law Jethro called him out on it. After Moses sent his family back to the in-laws because he couldn't sustain leadership with his family around, Jethro brings Moses' family back to him. He asked Moses, "Why do you sit alone while all the people sit and stand around you from morning until evening?"

Jethro proceeded to challenge Moses to share the load. The job was simply too big, so Jethro recommended a leadership structure and some needed layers of organization that would ultimately save Moses from a certain melt down and likely free up space for him to do what he and the people of Israel really needed—to pursue God in extended ways.

If we read the story carefully, we see the indicators. There were signs in Moses' life that he was headed for trouble. Let's look at them.

- Earlier in Exodus 14, Moses sent his wife and sons back home. Apparently, he was unable to do his job with his family around; a sure sign of problems on the horizon.
- It became increasingly obvious that Moses was isolated and trying do more and more of the leadership completely on his own.
- The way Moses approached leadership wasn't good for the people he was leading. People waited long hours for him to settle disputes. Moses' modus operandi was inefficient and unsustainable.

Can you relate? Today drivenness, the pace of our culture, the role of technology, and the sheer weight of leadership is wreaking havoc. Anxiety and depression are at all-time highs in America, and not just among adults. We are modeling this fast-paced, constantly moving lifestyle to our kids, and their struggles with depression and anxiety and use of meds as an answer are at record levels. People, especially leaders, refusing to slow down, take time and refill their emotional and spiritual tanks is exacting a huge cost on families, organizations, and churches.

In the church alone we have all felt the disappointment when we hear stories of the affairs, failures, and struggles that have taken many great leaders down. Christian leaders too often burnout or flame out, charring churches and families in the process. For years in Harbor Ministries we cited the chilling statistics from research conducted in the early 2000s by the Barna Research

Group. At that time, 80 percent of seminary and Bible school graduates left their ministries within the first five years. Fifteen hundred pastors walked away from ministry every month due to moral failure, spiritual burnout, or contention in their churches. Fifty percent of pastors' marriages ended in divorce.

The statistics have improved some. Maybe we're getting a little wiser. A 2015-16 study conducted by the Francis A. Schaeffer Institute for Leadership Development found that pastors tended to be happier personally and more satisfied with their calling than their counterparts two decades earlier. Still, 35 percent of pastors reported they battle depression and 26 percent said they are overly fatigued. More than half say they are overworked and say they cannot meet the expectations of their churches. Forty-three percent are overstressed.

Millennial leaders, like the rest of their generation, are more likely to report they are stressed. A 2013 article in USA Today reported that while stress levels for Americans are declining, stress among Millennials is higher than the national norm. Fifty-two percent of Millennials surveyed said that stress keeps them awake at night. And, according to the American Psychological Association, Millennials (those born between 1982 and 2004) have a higher percentage of members who report they have been diagnosed with either depression or anxiety than any other age group.

Now there are numerous reasons spiritual leaders struggle today, but a big one is the failure of leaders to set a sustainable pace for life and leadership, plus their failure and the failure of others to recognize the indicators of fatigue and burnout along the way. When we were just starting our Rhythm in Twenty groups, we took out an ad in a national magazine that showed a young leader, alive and well, lying in a coffin. It resonated with leaders who had people pressing in on them, who couldn't escape their lists, computers, phones, and messages.

Brian was one of the young leaders who responded to that ad. We selected

Brian for the Harbor program because he was making things happen. He was doing youth ministry at a very high level, and influencing many teens and other leaders throughout the Southeast. What I did not expect was the look I saw in Brian's eyes the first night of our very first gathering. He had a desperate look, a look that said, "I badly need to see God. I need Him to meet me through this experience, or I am not sure I can make it any further."

Brian came halfway across the country to join twenty others on a journey that he knew very little about. He just knew he needed to change how he was living and how he was doing ministry. He was living at an absolutely unsustainable pace. Pure fatigue was about to take him out. I was shocked by Brian, but I shouldn't have been. If I would have looked in the mirror a few years earlier I might have seen that haunted look in my own eyes. Looking back, I can see now how I missed the indicators that were revealing the depths of the fatigue that nearly cost me everything.

- I was playing less.
- I was praying less.
- Little things were setting me off much more easily than usual.
- I had an increasing need for escape. This was different than separating from work.
- More of my identity was becoming tied to my work.
- I had stopped reading and learning. I was not stretching myself anymore.
- I had pulled back from pursuing God in the quiet and extended times of solitude.
- I felt alone. It seemed like I had no leadership peers I connected well with.

Part of the problem for me was the nature of my work. As I felt the storm brewing, I didn't feel I had anyone to turn to, so I continued to throw myself into the work in front of me while fatigue took hold under the surface.

RUNNING A SMART RACE

Watching my sons' track meets through the years provided a clear illustration of what it means to run the race well and have something left in the tank to finish strong. My youngest son was a gifted track athlete and he excelled in several events, but it was a not-so-successful relay race his sophomore year that I remember vividly. Dylan was running the second leg of the race. He received a great handoff and after the first lap he was well out in front. The problem was, he forgot that he was on an indoor track and would be running two laps that day. On the back stretch of the second lap he hit the proverbial wall. As he came into the last turn he faded, struggling to make the handoff. The relay team finished last that day.

Dylan was at his best in the 110-meter high hurdles. He had the eighth fastest time in the state as a freshman, and would have been a favorite to be a state champion had it not been for the sports hernia injuries that plagued him later in high school. I learned the most watching him run those hurdles. Each stage of that fast race is equally important. You must start well and stay close to the lead in the middle hurdles. Then you need energy, passion, and enough competitive fuel in the tank to land strong off the last hurdle and sprint toward the finish line.

THE START

Watching Dylan convinced me that no matter the distance of the race, the start is always critical. It sets the tone for the entire race. But it's not just about that moment; it's about the preparation, training, diet, and rest. It's about harnessing the passion and drive that will get you out of the blocks fast, and give you the kind of start necessary for a good race.

As you read this, think about something new you are starting. It might be a relationship, a ministry, a project at work, or even a new season of life. What are some of the keys to a successful first stage of this race? Are you prepared? Are you focused? Is your mission clear? Do you have the passion that will drive you out of the blocks and sustain you through the race? Are you continuing to lay the foundation to help you run well? Is there anything you need to change, shift, or adjust as you start the race?

We must be careful not to come out of the blocks too fast. So often in my life I've started things with great passion and come strong out of the blocks, only to drop off the pace and lose heart and energy when things get tough. In terms of your pursuit of God, your work, ministry, relationships, family, and your personal world, are you running at a pace you can sustain for the duration of the race? With some of the current challenges in my life lately, I'm reminded that if don't want to burnout, if I am going to have enough fuel in the tank to finish this next stretch, well, I had better remember that every day, every moment, every stage of the race counts.

THE MIDDLE

We rarely talk about the middle of the race but it can be the difference maker. The middle of the race is where the men are separated from the boys, where the rubber meets the road, where we fight the hardest, for the longest, for the most important things. In the middle of the race we need to be reminded of our goal. We need hope.

I think about the countless moments the Israelites spent in exile wondering if they would ever make it to the Promised Land. Think about the relative silence of those forty years. Think about how incredibly hard it had to be for Moses and the other leaders to keep the people focused, inspired, encouraged, taking the next steps, facing the next day, the next month, the next year, and not lose hope. I think about Paul and how that man somehow found great satisfaction and impact even in prison and amid violence and oppression. I think about Christ on the cross, feeling abandonment in ways we'll never know. The Israelites, Moses, Paul, and even Christ were all in the middle of the race, somehow fighting to tread the water that lies in the middle. It's in the middle that we must remind ourselves again and again what race we're running and why we are running it in the first place. It's the time when weariness, burnout, and fatigue set in. It's the time when we forget the why and just continue going through the motions.

Beware that the middle is often where boredom sets in. What are you in the middle of? What races are you in where you feel like you're running out of the passion and energy you need to keep going? Are you tired? Bored? Be honest with yourself. Are you spiritually tired of fighting the good fight? Tired of doing your best and wondering if it's ever good enough? Tired of all the doing and wondering where and how you are going to fill the tank so that you can take the next steps, and lean into the next adventure and challenge God may have for you?

In the middle of Moses' leadership journey, he risked losing everything. Think what the impact would have been if Moses had burned out. An entire nation was depending on him to lead them through a long, draining, trying time in the wilderness. It took a lot for Moses to realize he was in trouble. He had to be teachable and allow his father-in-law Jethro to insert himself into his life and leadership. Jethro confronted Moses and gave him a plan that included trusting others, passing off some leadership duties, and creating a structure that would help Moses manage the incredible complexities of leadership. If Moses had not made this midlife correction, if he had not taken the time to slow down, to pause and listen, if he had not been teachable and made some needed changes, there is no way he would have made it to the finish line.

So what struggles have you faced in the middle? What kind of pace have you been running? What have you perhaps forgotten, left behind, or missed along the way?

THE FINISH

Any great race has a beginning followed by many challenges in the middle, but it also has a definitive finish line. As I watched my son finish strong in one race after another, I noticed that he always had his eye on the finish line. Because there is a finish line, right? In this next season of life, this job, this day, this month, this year, there is a finish line. To run this race well, we must remember that. This will help us to be, do, see, endure, and experience all the things God has for us, in the thin place moments and in the seasons, adventures, challenges, and callings that await us. This is true with a race, and it's true in life. We must create space, sustain a pace, and retain a passion for what we are doing that will allow us to stay the course and finish well.

In my family and work, I've tried my best to have the end in mind. The times I've failed to do this—and there have been many over the years—were the times I put my character, my reputation, my family, or myself at risk. Whether it is the daily moral and ethical decisions that each of us face in work, marriage, or other relationships, if we fade too quickly, if we fail to keep some fuel in the tank, it will cost us dearly. If we want to live life with rhythm and a freedom true to our values and convictions and in line with how God has wired us, if we want to be alert and ready to see and experience the thin moments along the way, then we had better attend to all stages of the race.

As I reflect on those awesome memories of my kids' track meets, I remember how much I enjoyed watching them compete, challenge themselves, and have fun. I am also reminded of some principles that hold true no matter what race we're running.

- Training, diet, preparation, passion, and will to win are so important.
- Maintain good form throughout the race.
- Sometimes you must slow down, control your breathing and set a pace that's appropriate for the race you're in. Don't get ahead of yourself.
- Stay relaxed.
- Be tough. Overcome the voices that scream at you to stop, slow down, or settle.
- Remember that the race is won when you attend to all of the stages.

So when it comes to finishing the next week, month, six months, year, five or ten years, what do you want the people who are walking with you to remember? How do you want to influence their lives? What are two or three things you would want others to know, see, or experience from having been around you? Or to put it even more simply, what are a few words that you would want others to take away from time spent with you? Take a moment now to write those words down.

What are a couple of bucket list items you want to make sure you have the time and energy for in the next season of life?

Is there anything that you need to make sure is in place to help you continue a passionate pursuit of God and set a healthy rhythm and pace going forward? Anything that comes to mind that would help you not miss those thin places along the journey?

All of this brings me back to an illustration I heard years ago. We all have spiritual, emotional and physical tanks and we must pay attention to the gauges—the indicators—and know when our tanks are getting low. We must also know how to refuel. So what fills my tank? What are some of the things that will keep me engaged spiritually? For a person who talks a lot about living and leading with great rhythm and balance in life, these last couple of months have not had much of either. Sometimes there are seasons when that is the case, but as much as I love what I'm doing now with Harbor Ministries, I must be proactive to avoid fatigue and weariness. I must be aware of what will give me the energy, the rest, and the refreshment I will need to bring my best to the next stretch of the race. Let me describe a day that recently filled my tank.

It started with a great bike ride, and then I met three of the guys from an earlier Rhythm in Twenty group at one of my favorite spots, the Starbucks in the REI store in downtown Denver. Getting with some guys who have been on a three-year leadership journey with us was a breath of fresh air. Catching up some on their lives and seeing the vision and spark in their eyes as they talked about what God is doing in their work and families was just what I needed. After a morning of connecting with these guys I felt refreshed and more prepared to step into the demands of the next week.

We must be involved in the things that re-energize and refresh us—things that fill our tanks. For me it was some deep connection with some guys I love investing in, a bike ride around a mountain lake, and some coffee at my favorite spot. Simple things that breathed life back into me.

If you are at a point of needing some vision, some energy, some passion for the weeks ahead, think about some things that are life-giving. Make a short list and then go for it. I'm seeing more than ever that if I'm going to effectively reach that next destination, I first have to do things that fill my tank along the way.

* * * * *

As I hit the wall, and as the perfect storm began to take hold in my life, what I remember most was how spiritually tired I felt. The weariness of my soul physically weighed me down. Fatigue absolutely played a central role in the near-total crash. I came out of a decade and a half of leading a large organization tired... so tired. I wasn't seeing things clearly. I was missing the thin places along the way. I was so tired that I simply was not hearing that still, small, quiet voice of God. I had lost my way. Fatigue gave way to anxiety and depression that took months, and the help of many, to emerge from. When leaders get tired so many things can happen. One of those things is that he or she can stop trusting their intuition, or gut. I'm a strong intuitive feeler. I tend to make a lot of my decisions on gut feelings. But when I get tired, it gets much more difficult to trust those feelings and intuitions, and it gets much easier to start to listen to other voices and influences. So much can happen when we are tired.

But this is the good news: Out of that dark time, the roots of a new ministry were planted. I had a dream, a literal dream, of creating a harbor. A place of depth. Protection. Refuge. A place to drop anchor and get refueled and recharged. A place where weary refugees could find rest. A place where leaders could reconnect with a deepening sense of mission. A place of equipping. A place of building up and tearing down. A place of listening and quiet. A place to drop anchor, but also a place to raise it and get moving again.

As I write tonight, there is this strong sense that there was a purpose for those tired and weary places I found myself in. As hard as it was at times to keep going, to keep pursuing God, to keep running in the middle part of the race, there was a sense that there was a reason for all of it. The storm of fatigue that nearly took me out actually deepened my understanding of God, and without a doubt it deepened the impact I've had through Harbor Ministries.

As we chased that crazy cliff in Iceland, it brought a sense of passion, energy, and hope. Those of us who took that journey will never forget the mission and purpose the adventure sparked in us. It filled our tanks. It gave us the finish—and the start—we needed for the next stage of the race.

DISAPPOINTMENT

In Iceland, before we went on these holy adventures each day, we gathered to reflect on the journey of Harbor Ministries and all the things that God has done. One morning we decided to talk some about the spiritual history of Iceland. This discussion was sparked by our visit to the tiny church where we found the Bible dated 1586 lying open on the pulpit.

That morning we read the story of one of the early missionaries who somehow felt the call to Iceland. Let's just say it: In the sixteenth century getting on a boat to cross the frigid North Sea to live and minister in Iceland... that was a crazy, out-of-control calling. Those early Celtic missionaries had to put everything on the line to reach these people.

Let's imagine what it may have been like. Our young Celtic monk boards a ship in England. The ship heads north into colder waters than he's ever experienced. He's not swimming, but he can tell from the biting ocean breeze. After he's been in Iceland a year, or three, or maybe ten, the thoughts swirl in his head. "Wait a minute. I'm living in Iceland. ICELAND! It's stupid-cold in the winter. I'm laying it all on the line for you, God, just like I thought you wanted. But nothing is happening."

In those long, dark, cold winter days the occasional disappointment had to be crippling. It had to be intense. It had to be discouraging. Our no-longer-so-young monk had to wonder if he had gone wrong. He had to question exactly where God was in this part of his story. But then there were thin place moments that likely got him and his co-conspirators through. Those extended times of seeing Gods beauty in that incredible place, and maybe those moments of impact that came along and gave him the energy he needed to keep going.

That's the kind of moment I wondered about as we searched for a lake in central Iceland that is fed by hot springs. It was a place those early missionaries took Icelanders who wanted to be baptized. We arrived at one-thirty in the morning and the midnight sun was fading. We were losing light, but were determined to find this lake that we had read and heard so much about. As we searched I thought about those baptisms. Those had to be some incredible moments all those years ago. It is not hard to imagine those frigid cold grayish days in the central mountains disrupted by celebrative moments of baptism in those warm waters. Those had to be thin place moments those early Christians would never forget—moments that helped those leaders stay the course when faced with seasons of disappointments, fatigue, and boredom.

We ran out of light and were unable to find the lake.

So, what do you do with disappointment? I mean real disappointment like our young monk experienced. Or the devastating disappointments my family has faced at times. What do you do with the kind of disappointment that makes you question everything? The dream-crushing, kick-in-the-gut kind that can leave you listless, apathetic, or worse.

It's a question I've thought a lot about during the last few years. It seems to be a constant theme in my life and in the lives of some of those closest to me— disappointment in myself, in life circumstance, in how some things have turned out. Disappointment in God.

When I was twenty-six my dad died of a heart attack. He was playing Santa Claus in a mall at the time, which was just one of the many ways he loved life and lived it to the fullest. He died on December 22nd. His funeral was on Christmas Eve. On the 26th, we were supposed to leave for Florida to go to a college football bowl game, then enjoy a day of deep sea fishing before meeting the rest of the family for a Caribbean cruise. The trip never happened.

My dad was a farmer in central Nebraska. He loved the land, but loved the people more. In so many ways he was the rudder of our family—steady, unwavering, consistent, unconditional in his love for us. It's been more than thirty years since his death, but his quiet strength, fervent pursuit of fun, faith, and family continues to deeply impact me and what I do to this day. If there was anything good that came from that event all those years ago, it was that it launched me down the road of writing. Journaling was the best way for me to deal with the grief.

Life continued to move fast. We had a son a few months after my dad died, and our daughter a couple of years after that. A few years later my mom found cancer. After battling the crushing disease for several years, she lost the fight. There I was. A father of three, now thirty-three years old, and both my parents were gone. It was difficult to process my loss and disappointment. My journals were filled with many more questions than answers.

The last few months of my mom's life were rough as the cancer spread through her body. We drove a couple of hours to see her, thinking it might be our last visit. But she rallied and after a few days, we drove home and I went back to work. A week later I had a sense that I should go see her, and a good friend of mine felt the same thing. But that same night a crisis developed at the Youth for Christ ministry I was directing, and I decided to head to Kansas City to help our staff resolve the issues. On the drive down, I pulled over at the Hamburg, Iowa exit and sat in my car immobilized, trying to decide whether to head back to see my mom or drive on to Kansas City. After an hour of indecision and struggle I headed to Kansas City. My mom died the next day.

More than two decades later, when I drive by that exit, I still feel the sense of failure and disappointment in myself. It's not as painful as it used to be, but it still triggers emotion every time.

That had to be some of what Peter experienced the morning after Jesus was arrested. Just hours before, Jesus had warned Peter that he would deny knowing him three times. Peter had to be thinking, "There is absolutely no way! After all we've been through, after the miracles and all I've seen Jesus do, there is no way I will deny him." Yet here he sits, the rooster crowing just after Peter denied knowing Jesus on three different occasions. It's hard to imagine the level of failure, despair, and disappointment Peter must have felt in himself. In the days that followed, and probably for the rest of his life, Peter had to wince every time he heard a rooster crow. It had to trigger an emotional and physical reaction.

As I passed by this exit a few years ago I remembered again that moment of sitting there in my car. I remember thinking that I did not want to see my mom in her deteriorating condition again. It was so hard to watch her suffer and to be reminded of the unanswered prayers that had been a part of this journey. Just a few years ago, I was still processing the profound disappointment as I wrote in my journal.

October 5, 2015

So, twenty-one years ago my mom died. Such perspective on how fast time flies.

Such perspective on how young I was when that happened.

What was the loss of parents so young all about, I wonder?

Life goes so fast it really is important to not get stuck, not waste too much time in negativity. There are so many questions, there is so much to ask God.

But this I know, the woman pursued God until the end. She had a soft heart and reached out to so many in her short time on earth. She sang, she served, she loved unconditionally...

Last night I drove by the exit on the way to Kansas City where I pulled over twenty-one years ago. I sat there and wondered if I should go to K.C. and work, or go to Grand Island and see my mom again in her last days. I sat there for an hour and then drove on to K.C. ...one of the great mistakes of my life.

How did I not hear God more clearly that night? One day later she died. What a moment missed. I can feel the emotion and weight of that build even now. I am so sorry for that. To the best of my ability, I swore to not make that kind of selfish mistake again. Determined not to miss the key moments, determined and resolute—my commitment to put relationship first and I've tried my best since then.

Peter must have faced some of the same feelings. That disappointment weighs on me still. You can feel it in between the lines of my journal. As the Hamburg exit so often reminds me, disappointment and regret can have real impact on our lives over the long haul. But it also reminds me that if we look disappointment square in the eye and name it, deal with, and not cover it up, some good can come from the pain.

Some of my favorite words in the Bible are found in Psalm 73 and 77. I love the author Asaph. He just put it out there. He said what he was feeling. He was painfully honest. He had what seemed like significant swings of passion and despair. He clearly was a feeler, which I can relate to. You get the sense that he was in a wrestling match with God over life's circumstances—more of a boxing match, I think. You can feel his anger, sadness, disillusionment, and his hurt.

But somehow, each of these psalms takes an amazing turn. Asaph's perspective seems to change and the tone becomes hopeful instead of desperate. How do you explain the shift that occurs? In a lot of ways, it doesn't make any sense. Was he just writing it to make a point? Was his intent all along to just write something dramatic and then end it on a spiritual note? Did Asaph experience one of those elusive thin place moments as he wrote Psalm 73:

> Surely in vain I have kept my heart pure... for I have been stricken all day long and chastised every morning. When I pondered to understand this, it was troublesome in my sight until I came into the sanctuary of God. Then I perceived their end.
> Psalm 73:13-17 (NASB)

From that point on the whole psalm changes. Whatever happened in the sanctuary, whatever the sanctuary was, and however long it took, things changed after that encounter. Asaph goes on to write,

> *Whom have I in heaven but you, and besides you, I desire nothing*
> *on earth. My flesh and my heart may fail, but God is the strength of my*
> *heart and my portion forever.*
>
> Psalm 73:25-26 (NASB)

So, I ask myself, and I ask you again, what do we do with disappointment? I know everyone reading this has walked this road. Do you cover disappointment with petty churchy answers? Do you bury it, ignore it, or try and escape from it? Do you minimize it? Or do you wrestle with God, like Asaph did?

It's easy to get frustrated and feel guilty when disappointment sets in. We tell ourselves all kinds of things:

- There are worse things.
- Other people are going through much tougher things than I am.
- I shouldn't let this get me down.
- Why do I feel stuck?
- That just must be what God wanted.
- It's not right to be brutally honest with God about how I feel. I just need to suck it up.

It's so easy to minimize this emotion and what results from it, but I can tell you that's not a good idea. I let disappointment eat at me and it contributed in a big way to my midlife crash. My son Dylan struggled with injuries that ended his basketball dreams. Even as I write this I sense myself minimizing it, thinking there is no way this journey should be this hard. So many parents and families are walking through very tough stuff with their kids. Some families are facing life and death issues with their kids. Get a grip, Tim. This is not that bad.

But I want to lean into this and share this story partly because it has been a difficult struggle with deep disappointment over many years. In some ways, it still has a grip on me. This is the kind of disappointment that, if we don't recognize it and deal with it, can eventually take us out. At the very least they will take a toll. It is the kind of thing that an enemy can leverage against us.

Basketball has been a big part of our family. My dad was a talented college player who loved the game. I have a picture my aunt gave me of his college team playing the Harlem Globetrotters. So many of my earliest memories with him were going to high school and college games, and watching the UCLA Bruins or the L.A. Lakers on TV. I grew up with a passion to play basketball, and though I wasn't as good as my dad, I loved the game. Our three kids all had great moments playing the sport. We were blessed to watch them all challenge themselves and play in competitive environments through high school.

But our youngest son was different. His first word was ball. From early on, he had a basketball with him 24/7. He had the gift to play basketball at an exceptional level and that's not just a biased dad talking. Others began to talk college basketball with him as early as middle school. Just recently I was watching a kid play for Oklahoma State and my mind raced to Dylan playing against that young man in a national tournament in middle school. Dylan got the best of him that day.

Dylan's talent was obvious, but so was his desire to use the platform that athletics was giving him to show God's love to others. His dream was to play Division 1 basketball and have an even bigger platform to demonstrate what a relationship with God could do.

The opportunities to display his talent were growing. Before his junior year in high school he was playing at AAU tournaments around the country. College coaches were taking notice and the exciting, high-adrenaline experience of recruiting had begun. He carried the momentum of that summer into his junior year. He was scoring more than thirty points in some games, and his dream school, the University of Nebraska, invited him to a few practices. He broke the single-game scoring record for his school and was featured in the sports section of our local paper. It was an exciting time.

Just a few days later Dylan was injured. It happened during a personal workout at home after a big game. He heard and felt something pop. The next day he could barely walk. What followed were countless doctor and physical therapy appointments, and an intense spiritual battle.

I could feel the weight right away. I knew this was more than a physical injury. I remember being on the floor in my office each morning, feeling overwhelmed as I prayed for Dylan. I asked God for healing. I asked him to honor this kid who so much wanted to honor God with his talent. I asked God to let him enjoy this incredible moment that was in front of him. But the difficulty continued. The healing did not come. We were on the front end of a season of deafening silence from God.

Dylan returned to play three weeks later, in a lot of pain, but determined to finish the year strong and will his team to the state playoffs. But the obstacles he faced were big, and the year that started with the promise of a push for a state championship and the dream of college recruiting, ended in crushing disappointment. The playing field had changed and what would define wins and losses was different now.

The following summer Dylan had sports hernia surgery the same day he was supposed to be playing in a national tournament in Las Vegas. Disappointment took root.

Even though he held it well, disappointment was taking root in Dylan's life as its roots were growing deeper in mine. My journals were filled with struggle and questions. It was likely a blessing in disguise that I lost the journal I had kept that summer. It was almost as if God was saying, "You needed to write and process this journey for sure, but I am not going to let you get stuck there."

As Dylan headed into his senior year, hope was restored. The issues and the long frustrating summer seemed to be behind him, but within the first couple weeks of practice, it became clear that there was a continuing problem. We were living under a crippling cloud of frustration and disappointment, as we knew he was likely facing another surgery.

After much research, I had found a surgeon in Germany that specialized in in sports hernia surgeries like Dylan needed, with a promised quick recovery. The surgery was on December 20th in Germany. Weeks later Dylan was back on the court. I think we all thought a redemptive story was playing out, and his platform of influence was growing.

He played his senior season, and there were so many fun and amazing moments in the weeks following the surgery. The local media covered the story of his trip to Germany, and so many others were encouraged by Dylan's testimony and how he communicated his faith through the pursuit of his basketball dream. A few weeks later his coach talked about how inspiring Dylan's trip to Germany was. A father and son pursuing what they believed God was calling them to was something he would never forget.

But as his senior season ended, the pain was becoming worse. Even though none of us wanted to admit it, Dylan's dreams were being dismantled again. A third surgery followed. Three tryouts with his dream school all ended in disappointment due to his physical limitations. It's been a long frustrating journey with pain that Dylan's still on today. I wrote this just a few months ago, as we headed to visit yet another doctor in Florida, four years after he graduated from high school.

January 29, 2017

Why so hard still? So much emotion... so much weightiness when I think of Dylan's journey.

One thought of what could have been in track today:

So gifted yet so blocked from using that gift again and again.

Opportunities come and then are taken away... and still today he is not better. He still deals with pain.

Why is this so heavy for me? Why so hard?

He would have used that platform in such a powerful way. I just don't understand it.

I prayed diligently and fervently. I felt it was a spiritual thing from the beginning and prayed aggressively, but it seemed like those prayers were met with silence and disappoint again and again.

Why has God seemed so quiet through all these years?

The only thing I can think of is that I carried this heavy burden so Dylan did not have to. My disappointment is so intense... maybe it somehow took some of the weight off him because he has been amazing. He never seemed to doubt God through any of it. Steady, hurting, but positive through all of it.

But for me the disappointment, the anger... the sense of loss is still crushing.

As Dylan and I visited a specialist in Florida, and as we hoped that maybe this would be the thing that finally fixed Dylan's issues, I still struggled. I doubted God. I doubted the decisions we'd made for Dylan, and I started to slide into disappointment. Then a thin place came out of nowhere. After separating to explore the town of St. Augustine, I came across a small historic church. Feeling compelled to go in, I heard the last few words of the priest who was just ending the daily mass. "Sometimes faith is just hanging on. But if we continue to pursue a relationship with Jesus throughout our lives, just maybe we can do more than hang on. Maybe we can do more than survive during the hardest of times. Maybe we can actually thrive during those times."

I turned around to go outside and capture what he had said on my phone, and I read this on a sign in front of that church. "We have been a faith community that has endured many difficult times and by entering these doors you join a church family that has stood the test of time..." As best I remember, it said the church had deep roots. It was founded in 1584, making it the oldest established church in America. In a matter of five minutes God had given me words that I really needed, some of them on a sign that had most likely been in place decades before the moment I would need to read them.

A few days later some perspective came as I experienced another quiet thin place moment as I sat on the beach. I was journaling and the angry words, discouraging words, helpless words poured out. Then, like Asaph's psalms, the tone shifted. The words from that tiny church resonated, and I had a moment of turning, a moment when I found a glimpse of hope and truth.

February 9, 2016

St. Augustine, FL

The question begs to be asked... what has this journey been about? This journey that has taken us all over the country and all over the world. Surely it is about more than just basketball.

Why has God allowed this to happen?

Why has he remained so silent with literally years of unanswered prayer?

Why have Dylan's hopes been built up and dashed again, and again?

The way this has played out seems cruel.

Dylan remains faithful, seeking God... others are watching him. Can God not reward him by intervening? By somehow rewarding his faithfulness?

How do you process lost opportunities, the hundreds of hours of recovery and rehab, and the continual reminders of the deep disappointments along the way? And how in the world do you process God's role in the day-to-day of this? As I sit here, on the edge of frustrations and a disheartened and lost hope, thoughts begin to come... I am urged to remember and capture some truths along the way...

A few things I know for me:

1) I have relentlessly prayed and sought God on this, yet this season has been filled with what seems like unanswered prayer and unending times of silence. It has been a struggle to keep pursuing Him through all of this. Yet I have tirelessly done just that. This journey has kept me close and in an intense, honest, raw pursuit of God.

2) There is something to me carrying the weight of disappointment, anger, frustration to God... something in the role of a father carrying this weight emotionally and spiritually. It seems that it is something I could carry so that Dylan's load was a bit lighter.

3) I must journal and be totally honest about how I am processing this. So, God... let's do this again. I'm frustrated, I'm angry, and I need to keep writing and keep processing this in this journal.

A few things I know for Dylan:

1) He is much deeper, more compassionate, more tuned in, and his heart for God has been incredible and unwavering. He will no doubt be a steady post, an anchor, a captain for others when they go through rough waters.

2) There is a weightiness to his life that is different. Others gravitate to him even more than they did before.

3) Maybe he is learning more of what he wants to be about and how he wants to help people going forward. I'm hoping he learns to trust his gut, his intuitions...

Now I would like to say that as a dad, I was calm, always leading well, and reassuring others that God was present through all this journey with Dylan. While that was sometimes true of me, there were many dark moments. I wanted to believe there was a bigger reason this was happening, and to say that I had a sense of peace through the crazy and deeply disappointing journey. That was sometimes the case, but my journals reveal the frustration, anger toward God, confusion, and honestly, downright despair at times.

I know the right spiritual answers and all the right things to say, but so much of that is not working anymore. On more than one occasion, God and I had it out. I struggled with feeling like I had screwed it up, and had made some wrong decisions for Dylan. But through all of this, I must admit, I have never been closer to God, more in touch with this journey of faith, or with difficult journeys of others.

Maybe because of my own journey of disappointment I am very keen to the disappointments of others, particularly those that involve basketball. Of all the great games and significant moments in the 2014 March Madness tournament, one really captured my attention. It was the plight of Wichita State, and the comments of their coach after the game. Wichita State was the first team in the history of the NCAA to go 35-0 in a single season. They played a much younger but very talented Kentucky team in one of the best games I have ever seen. The Wichita State Shockers seemed to play flawlessly, but lost. One play, one shot, one moment could have made all the difference and may well have propelled them to a perfect season... the kind of season that may never have been matched. That may be hard for those players to shake.

It was not the game as much as the scene from their locker room that has stuck with me. It evoked some emotion and a very familiar theme; disappointment. Crushing disappointment was evident in the hollow eyes and sagging shoulders of those kids who had accomplished so much. It brought back painful reminders of my struggle over the last couple of years. In those faces I saw the danger of letting disappointment settle in. Unchecked, disappointment can overwhelm and impact our perspective on life. The Shockers' coach told his players how proud he was of what they had accomplished. He exhorted them to remember that they had put together the most successful run in the history of college basketball, and he pleaded with them to know that they had nothing to hang their heads about. I hope they took his words to heart.

I've realized a few things about disappointment over the last couple of years. Perhaps these words can help as you face some of the disappointments that life throws your way.

- I need to name it, feel it, and express it. Burying disappointment does only damage.

- I must find that place to be totally real with it.

- It can be a key tool of an enemy who wants to turn me away from God.

- It can also be the starting place of needed restoration and hope.

- We have an enemy hell-bent on stealing, killing, and destroying. For me, one of the easiest ways that can happen is to get stuck in the journey of disappointment.

- I can't let disappointments bury me and wreck my faith. I cannot let it remain unresolved and unchecked. If they are allowed to build up, their combined weight will surely sink the ship.

So, what do we do with disappointment? If we don't deal with it, bring it to the surface, and lean into the incredible obstacles that crushing disappointment presents in our lives it will certainly bring us down.

More than anything else the events of these last few years have shown me that God walks with us through all life throws at us. He somehow broke through in profound, unexpected ways. My journey has shown me that He does in fact meet us in the darkest and hardest places.

2

PART TWO THE HOW

CHASING CLIFFS

Throughout these past few decades as I've been leading, succeeding, failing, hoping, and dreaming, I've discovered a few things along the way. First, I am made to chase cliffs. I need risks. My soul is wired for adventure. I'm compelled to find the edge then take one more step. When I stop doing this, my soul shrinks and I become less than God intended.

I needed to go to Iceland to engage in some key disciplines that would fuel me for the next season of life. I desperately needed:

To remember.

To lighten my load.

To become alert to the movement of God.

To awaken my soul.

To get space.

Through these intentional acts, I positioned myself to discover the thin places along the way.

REMEMBER

There is incredible power in remembering. I once heard John Eldredge say that a key tool of the enemy is forgetfulness. I think that's true. The further we separate ourselves from our powerful encounters with God, the more the memories of His tangible presence fade, the more likely we are to settle and to coast to the finish line. When we forget, we lose our passion and our effectiveness.

We went to Iceland to remember. The cliff had been our vision in the early days of Harbor Ministries. Now, it represented all that God had done through this movement. As we changed our pace and slowed down on those quiet mornings in the remote areas of Iceland, the stories flowed. When we took time to recall and retell them, our souls were sated and our strength renewed.

We revisited the early dream of Harbor Ministries, our crazy belief that we could actually change the world just twenty leaders at a time. A belief that if we can deeply invest in those who dare come into the Harbor, their lives, families, marriages, churches, and places of influence could be different. And as that kind of transformational change took place, the waves of influence would spread and change everything. It was the passion that drove me in those early days and still does.

There was Trevor, a pastor from the south who was the first guy to arrive at the lodge for our very first Harbor group. He sat in a chair nervously waiting for others to arrive, hoping he wasn't the only one crazy enough to fly across the country and take a chance on a new type of leadership experience. We laughed as we remembered that his wife was worried we were a cult. Then emotion came as we recalled how God met Trevor in a dark place and showed him a new way forward. Trevor now leads a large church and influences people in a different and deeper way.

Jason, a pastor from the East Coast, took a chance and joined a three-year journey that he knew very little about because he sensed God's presence in the process of applying. He was tired. He had felt deep loss, disappointment, and betrayal from those serving with him. He was overwhelmed by the needs of the people he was serving. In so many ways he felt isolated and alone. He entered the Harbor journey and something began to happen. As he quieted down, listened, and began to practice some new rhythms and create space in his journey, God showed up. Jason is a different man today and the story of the church he leads is radically different as a result.

I remember having a vision of Jason sitting beside the drummer boy in the "Glósóli" music video. I imagined the boy leaning over and whispering to Jason, "You can go climb that mountain and I will be with you. If you just want to sit here and be in awe of the beauty around us, I am with you. If you want to be still and do nothing for now, to rest up and re-engage your soul some, I'm here. You don't have to be busy. You don't have to be accomplishing anything to sense my presence. No matter what you are doing, I'm with you and I'm proud of you."

Even as I write about that image of Jason and the drummer boy, the truth of those words are deeply impacting. Jason needed that. I need that. We all need that.

In the vast, quiet spaces of Iceland we reminisced about the many things that have happened in our own lives as we've led the Harbor movement, including the heartaches, obstacles, and struggles we've encountered during this journey. Looking back, we see clearly the opposition of an enemy who never wanted us to launch Harbor and was determined to keep us from chasing that cliff.

There is so much depth, so much power in the simple practice of taking time to remember.

I have mentioned Asaph before. Asaph seemed to live, lead, and write with his gut and his intuition. In Psalm 77 he was in a desperate place. He was tired, frustrated, disappointed, and angry at people and God. In the early part of the psalm, he seemed despairing and almost hopeless. Psalm 77:2 (NASB) says, "In the day of my trouble I sought the Lord; In the night, my hand was stretched out, without weariness; My soul refused to be comforted."

Psalm 77:4, "...I am so troubled that I cannot speak."

Psalm 77:9, "Has God forgotten to be gracious, or has He in anger withdrawn his compassion?"

Then, in Psalm 77:11 everything changes. In what seems like a moment, Asaph's perspective shifts. What happened? He remembered. Read verse 11, "I shall remember the deeds of the Lord; Surely I will remember your wonders of old. I will meditate on all your work."

Asaph's writing was transformed by the simple discipline of remembering. Psalm 77:13-15: "Your way, O God, is holy; What god is great like our God? You are the God who works wonders; You have made known your strength among the peoples. You have by Your power redeemed Your people."

Wow, what a moment in the Bible. What a moment in Asaph's life. What a change took place through the power of remembering.

DO WE PLAY A PART?

I want to pause for a moment to discuss why I think remembering, among other disciplines, is related to this idea of God revealing himself in thin places. Remembering, lightening our burden, and remaining alert and awake incline our hearts toward God. I believe they make us aware of moments that we might otherwise miss.

Clearly, those times when heaven and earth collide—those brief moments when we get a glimpse into God's character, and we hear His whispers—those times and places are at His discretion and direction, but in some crazy way, do we play a role in creating those moments? I think of Moses and that burning bush. Within that story, the text says that when God saw Moses turn to the burning bush, He spoke. It is flat out mind blowing to think that God waited for Moses to turn before He spoke. Had He been there for days or years, just waiting for Moses to turn? I wonder.

Or those days after the crucifixion. It had to be an unbearably disheartening and disorienting time. Jesus had died, yet the disciples waited together, not knowing what to do, but likely hoping and maybe remembering that Jesus had promised to send a helper. He had told them that after His death someone would come who would be with them always, even to the ends of the earth. Someone who would be with them through life's trials, struggles, and heartbreaking disappointments. With them through the grief and loss that happens in this life. With them as they would sort through the opportunities and complexities of life and the calling that would follow. Even with them when they faced the ultimate darkness of an enemy who wanted to crush them. And when that holy wind blew through that room, they were present, ready, and waiting together in that hope.

I've mentioned Paul before. He was heading out of Jerusalem when he was stopped in his tracks. He had a thin place encounter so intense that everything changed as a result. God showed up and Paul was literally hit in the face and blinded. Can you imagine how his traveling companions must have reacted? Paul, this man so determined to wipe these Jesus followers from the face of the earth, had to enter utter darkness before he got to a place where he could really see. That can be so true with us. Sometimes it just has to happen that way. Sometimes God intervenes dramatically and directly. Sometimes He must hit us in the face and knock us down to get us to pay attention, to change course, and to go the direction that He has for us. But here's the hard part. Many times, it's impossible for us to see all of that in the moment. All we know is that we're blind, and lost, and hurting, and most likely pissed off that our plans have been disrupted. It is so important for us to remember that there is always more to the story playing out than what we see.

That's been the case in my life for sure. As I emerged from my midlife crisis and set out to finally launch this dream of a harbor, I was hit in the face and knocked back. I never would have guessed that I would first need to enter the harbor myself, before I could ever lead others into that journey. In a way,

I entered several months of blindness. For me, it was a wall of depression, quietness, and struggle. God led me to the edge of the cliff and asked me time and time again if a relationship with Him would be enough. If I could not lead others or launch this initiative, if I lost the things that I'd worked so hard for, would God still be enough?

Those thin place moments when God disrupts business as usual and changes the trajectory of my life often seem to manifest themselves at places where His work and my awareness and readiness to respond intersect. There seems to be an allusive mix of God's power and my sweat.

This is not a new concept. Countless books, songs, and sermons have been spoken through the generations pleading with us to listen, to seek God, to follow Him. It makes me wonder if there are, in fact, some things we can and should do to better align ourselves with the thin places when they show themselves.

LECTIO DIVINA

In all of our Harbor leadership events, we participate in Lectio Divina, an ancient practice of meditating repetitively on scripture. It is the idea of letting God's word read us, soak in, and, as a result, deeply impact us instead of the other way around. It's amazing how often God breaks through the third or fourth time we read a passage. I've experienced it myself and seen it happen many times for others. Eugene Peterson describes this ancient practice, likely used by many of those Celtic warriors in their times of solitude this way: "Lectio Divina is more Bible basking than Bible Study, as it teaches you to absorb and meditate on Scripture, to converse with God openly, and to live out what has become a part of you—His word."

"But it's not easy. Lectio Divina takes practice, and lots of it. You will have to learn to be quiet, to silence the voices of responsibility, self, family, and even religion in order to hear what God has to say to you."

We practice Lectio Divina in the leadership events in Harbor by starting with a slow, deliberate reading of a passage. Then we challenge our leaders to be still and quiet with the words as we read it a second time. Before we read the passage a third time, we ask for them to listen for that word or phrase that God may be uniquely speaking to them. We read the passage again, then invite them to speak aloud that word or phrase. We read the passage a fourth time and leave some moments of silence to let those words sink in one last time. One morning during one of our Lectio Divina readings, the words sunk in at a new level for me.

We were reading 1 Kings 8:56-58. I have heard this passage read countless times in our Harbor gatherings, but that morning, on the third reading, the word signposts stuck out to me. I sensed God saying, "You know what to do. I've already told you. You know it to be true. It's as if it's on a signpost. So go do it." A moment of clarity and direction came in the midst of a practice; the practice of me quieting down, slowing my pace, and letting those verses sink in. It seems I was a bit more ready to experience Him in the way I needed to that day. And in the moment, God asked me to remember. He wanted me to recall what I already knew. "You know what to do. I've already told you."

As I reflected on the passage in 1 Kings, the word signposts continued to resonate, and I began to recount some of the markers along my spiritual pilgrimage. I created a list of those signposts, those moments when God reminded me that He is real and that He has been with me along the way. I don't want to forget those moments when I have stood with Him on holy ground.

I've recounted stories of how God met me on a mountain outside of Quito,

Ecuador, and sent a messenger to me on a boardwalk in San Diego. Below I've listed some of the other places where God has met me, re-filled my tank, or put the wind back in my sails. These have been some of the places the Wild Goose just flat out showed up out of nowhere.

TRAIL 401 NEAR CRESTED BUTTE, COLORADO

For several years I've biked down this trail in Crested Butte, Colorado. Right above Gothic Pass, you have to push your bike up a single-track trail. After an aggressive stretch through a meadow, you emerge through some trees, and can see for miles down the valley to Crested Butte. On the other side, if you climb a little higher, you can see the Maroon Bells, two stunning mountain peaks that never fail to take my breath away. It's one of my favorite spots. For some reason, I think more clearly there.

I have had many great moments with friends and with God at the top of that trail. I came to somewhat of a peace with the loss of my parents there, and caught ideas regarding my future. I feel closer to God and more in His presence on that mountain top. The trail winds through open rock fields as it descends from above timberline, through aspen forests, creeks, and springs, past abandoned cabins, and meadows of wild flowers. You ride through a stream and weave around dense pine forests. Some of the real beauty is found down in the valley, but the view from up high is hard to beat.

COWBOY CHURCH

When I feel the need to reconnect with God, I usually head to the mountains. But one summer, I'd reached a point where I didn't even want to go to the high country. For me, that was a new low. But after the prodding of my wife and the encouragement of others, I headed west. I needed some time to try to get some

movement again in my relationship with God. And if there was more silence...
well at least I'd be in the mountains, right?

What I didn't expect was Cowboy Church.

I was on my way to one of my favorite spots, Hahns Peak north of Steamboat
Springs, Colorado. I decided to spend the night in Cheyenne, Wyoming. There
was maybe one room left in the city and it was right by the arena where Frontier
Days was going on. As I got up early Sunday to head out, I saw an invitation to
come to Cowboy Church in the arena where the rodeo was held. Cowboy Church
was not exactly on my agenda, but for whatever reason, I felt compelled to go.

For the third time in a couple of weeks I heard a talk on what faith looks
like when times are tough. The guy speaking said it's easy to have faith when
things are rolling, but what happens when times get tough, when life is unfair,
when disappointment sets in? I know. It's a message we've all heard before
many times, but it was also a message I'd been running from. I listened as he
said that faith only happens when we follow God, even when things make
no sense.

Real faith happens when we can't see. That was what I needed to hear and
God surprised me by delivering the message through Cowboy Church.

U2 CONCERT JUST MONTHS AFTER 9/11

It was a spontaneous trip to Kansas City that allowed this thin place to
happen. It was just a few weeks after 9/11 and the country was in mourning. Life
as we knew it had been disrupted by the attacks. As we entered the arena that
night something was different. There was the usual excitement and anticipation
that is always present at a U2 concert, but there was something else. Perhaps
the crowd and the country were looking for something deeper. I don't know if
Bono intended it or not (I suspect he did), but through the lyrics, the music,

and the moment, U2 connected me, a group of friends, and a crowd of 20,000 to something much bigger than ourselves. As the names of the first responders who had died trying to rescue others after the attacks rolled across the arena, U2 sang the haunting lyrics, "But I still haven't found what I'm looking for." Something in me screamed that we will always be in a relentless search for God this side of heaven. It became a night of flat out worship for me and my friends. It became one of the most memorable and impacting thin place moments in the last twenty years for me.

THE GRAND CANYON'S NORTH RIM

I don't have words to describe the awe and beauty of the place and the sense it gives me of how big the Divine Creator must be. If you haven't had the chance, you must experience this place. Go to the North rim away from most of the people, and sit on the edge of the rim at sunset. There just is nothing like it anywhere.

GOLD BEACH, OREGON

Just south of Gold Beach in southern Oregon, a trail winds its way to the ocean. It's an amazing place of awe-inspiring beauty. As I parked my car, there was this literal wall of fog just off the coast. It was like there was a dangerous, mysterious invitation that said, "Come check this out. You won't believe what you are going to see and experience." I entered the trail head and moved toward the rugged, dangerous coastline. The big surf was pounding the rocky shore below and I found myself in a place that beckoned me to enter in and to embrace reckless adventure.

THE JAMAICA BIKE TRAIL, FIVE MINUTES FROM MY HOUSE

I always feel a little bit better after a quick ride on this trail. From spring through the fall, I often have my bike strapped on the back of my jeep just in case I have a spare hour to hit this trail. Something in me settles down as I ride this trail. It has been a go to thin place for me for years.

A RANDOM APRIL NIGHT IN ESTES PARK

I experienced a mystical moment with my wife in Estes Park. It's hard to describe the collision of warm and cold, clouds and sun, darkness and light. The sun was setting over the mountains and it was snowing lightly from what seemed to be the clear sky above. We both paused, overwhelmed by the sense that we had been given a glimpse into something so much bigger.

These have been random, awesome, inspiring, encouraging, and often surprising moments—thin places that remind me that God walks through all of it with us. He is right there through the spectacular, through the mundane, and everything in between...

If we keep our eyes and ears open...

If we stay quiet enough...

If we practice listening...

If we will just take the time to remember...

God breaks through.

A WAY BACK

When we feel far from God, remembering can create a path back. David writes about this in Psalm 51. This was written after his ultimate failure, after this "man after Gods own heart" has fallen badly and is asking the questions so many of us ask: Where has God gone? Has he given up on me? Has He cast me aside? Is my story worth it anymore? Listen to David's words in Psalm 51:10-12 (NASB).

"Create in me a clean heart, O God, and renew a steadfast spirit within me. Do not cast me away from Your presence and do not take Your Holy Spirit from me. Restore to me the joy of Your salvation and sustain me with a willing spirit."

You can sense the desperate nature of this prayer. David was pleading for God not to abandon him, and in the middle of that desperate search, he asked for God to restore the joy of his salvation. He asked God to help him remember.

Do you remember the joy of your salvation, those early days when your faith was real and on fire? It's time to make your own list. When has God really surprised you? Where were you? Whom were you with? What were you doing? Now take a journal and find a way to go back to some of those places. Take the opportunity to remember that there is a bigger story playing out around you. I believe that if we lose sight of what we've experienced in those thin places, we will eventually fade or die spiritually. Remembering is important.

MOVING PAST THE PAST

Looking back is not enough. The power of remembering is in what it can do to propel us forward. Movement forward is the key. One August day, I found myself sitting on Coronado Beach in San Diego, a place where beauty collides with mission, passion, and purpose.

I watched Navy Seals training intensely for the critical unknown missions that awaited them. I also the saw the ships and sailboats pass by Point Loma and head out to open seas. Point Loma and the lighthouse there seem to both invite and point the way to the adventure—the risk, the mission, and the enjoyment of what lies beyond the safe harbor. Truthfully, I could have sat there all day and soaked it in. I could have enjoyed the beauty and been pretty content to stay on that beach and just think about what might lie beyond the harbor.

But as I sat there, it struck me that as critical as that time on the beach was—as important as it is to remember, to dream, plan, process and enjoy the moment—it was equally important to move forward, to step into whatever God had for me. I needed to be willing to step into the risk, the adventure, the mission, and the unpredictable moments that would await beyond the Point Loma lighthouse.

As I think about what lies ahead, the same is true. Dreaming, thinking, hoping, wondering what awaits me is important. The past has shown me that unpredictable highs and lows are likely ahead. There will be some adventure, some trials, some opportunities to trust God in even deeper ways. But just sitting, just remembering for the sake of remembering—not taking steps, not moving, just staying on the beach—cannot be an option. Life is just too short for that.

LIGHTEN

The Secret life of Walter Mitty is one of my favorite movies. Maybe it's because part of it takes place in Iceland, and I recognize some of the scenery, and have driven some of the roads shown on the screen. In the movie, Iceland represented so much for Walter as he began to understand and break down the barriers of his past. It represented the risks that he was willing to take, and it was the place where, for the first time, he began to slow down, soak in the moments, and realize it was much more about the journey than his ultimate destination. I loved this movie because I love Walter's story arc. This character who lived in a box, afraid to take risks, unwilling to step out, bored with his life and stuck in the heartbreak of his past began to see a way out.

Walter was a negative asset manager for *Life* magazine, which meant he managed and processed all the pictures that have made the magazine so captivating. As *Life* approached the publication of its last issue, they wanted to use a specific picture by one of their most prolific photographers on the cover, but there was a problem; Walter had lost the negative.

Now Walter must make a choice. I love the excitement he expresses when he finally decides to pursue the rogue photographer who had the negative he needed. The words, "The journey of a brave man" scroll across the screen. It takes courage to be willing to step out of your comfort zones. It takes bravery and determination to say, "I am not going to just settle in and coast." In Walter's case there was no guarantee he'd succeed, but he went anyway and the movie captures Walter's journey of slowly coming out of the box and discovering his true self.

His adventure began in Greenland where he got on a helicopter with a drunk pilot, jumped into the North Sea, fought off a shark, then had a fishing boat drop him off in Iceland. Along the way he began to shed unnecessary items. He left behind much of the baggage he'd brought with him. Some things he let go by choice, others by necessity. At one point, he traded something he'd been carrying for a longboard, then skateboarded down a windy road in Iceland, past hot springs, and waterfalls. The scenery was incredible and something amazing began to happen. Walter experienced freedom. You can see it. His countenance began to change as he rediscovered a passion from early in his life—a passion that had brought him joy before struggle and heartbreak began to take their toll. What made this transformational journey possible for Walter was that he let things go. He released some things that held him back both emotionally and physically.

Sometimes it is only when things are stripped away, when there is nothing we are carrying, no distractions, achievements, or accomplishment to block our view, that we find ourselves in thin places. Often we must lighten our load before we can experience God.

STRIPPED DOWN

When Dylan and I travelled to Germany for his hernia operation, we travelled light. We had just two days to plan for the trip. We stayed in a sparse, white room at a clinic on the edge of Munich. After the procedure, I was wide awake in the middle of the night. There was a snow storm raging, and a passing train disrupted any chance I had for sleep. I laid in bed thinking, "What have I done?"

I had failed to bring the proper electrical converters to charge our electronic devices. There was no one to talk to. Our nurse spoke very little English. It was a stripped down, vulnerable place, but in the sheer quiet of that surreal night, God spoke.

I spent some time writing in my journal.

December 20—

So here I sit in a doctor's clinic in Munich, Germany... struggling with doubt, struggling with fear, struggling to see God in the circumstances of this last year of Dylan's story. I'm struggling with questions.

Will this work?

Did we do the right thing in coming here?

...I have no idea and no certainty of the outcome here, yet there is a strange sense of clarity and peace that this was the next step we needed to take for Dylan. It wasn't just a crazy decision, I hope. Maybe the outcome will be physical and athletics will go the way we had hoped, but maybe there's way more to it than that. Maybe one of the

outcomes is the lesson that sometimes you do need to take steps into the darkness. Maybe he'll know and remember when he is twenty-five, or forty-five or sixty-five... Mostly though I think he'll remember we swung for the fence for him so he could continue to chase his dream. That alone is worth it.

As I finished my journal entry, God took my mind back to the story of Jonathan and his arms bearer and that moment when Jonathan says, "Perhaps God will be with us." Things changed in that instant. A sense came over me that seemed to say, "This is what you have done. You have entered into a risky trip with no guarantee of outcome. You have believed God led you to this place but you remain uncertain of the outcome. Tim, you have entered your own 'perhaps, God moment.'" My mind cleared and peace came over me. It's hard to explain, but God showed up, stirred a memory from the Bible and that changed the narrative of the story we were in.

In that moment there was nothing to distract me. As I think about what it takes to experience all that we were intended to experience in this life, and consider how we can live on mission ready to follow this mysterious God wherever he may take us, traveling light is critical. The lighter our load, the more easily we can react, shift, respond, and change directions as needed.

CAST OFF EVERYTHING THAT HINDERS

I have read, heard, and taught on Hebrews 12:1-3 many times over the years. Each time I read these words about how to run a smart race, I discover something new to think about and to process. Let's look at it from several versions of the Bible.

Cast off everything that hinders and the sin that so easily entangles and run with perseverance the race marked out for us. Keep your eyes on Jesus the author and perfecter of our faith, who endured the cross and the scorn of its shame. Keep your eyes on him so that you will not grow weary and lose heart.

Hebrews 12:1-3 (NAS)

Do you see what this means—all these pioneers who blazed the way, all these veterans cheering us on? It means we'd better get on with it. Strip down, start running—and never quit! No extra spiritual fat, no parasitic sins. Keep your eyes on Jesus, who both began and finished this race we're in. Study how he did it. Because he never lost sight of where he was headed—that exhilarating finish in and with God—he could put up with anything along the way: Cross, shame, whatever. And now he's there, in the place of honor, right alongside God. When you find yourselves flagging in your faith, go over that story again, item by item, that long litany of hostility he plowed through. That will shoot adrenaline into your souls!

Hebrews 12:1-3 (TM)

I love the imagery from the first line of this passage.

Let us strip off everything that slows us down... especially the sin that trips us...

Hebrews 12:1 (NLV)

...Throw off everything that hinders and the sin that easily entangles... and run with perseverance this race...

Hebrews 12:1-2 (NIV)

...lay aside every encumbrance...

Hebrews 12:1 (NAS)

We better get on with it, strip down, start running never quit... no extra spiritual fat... no parasitic sins.

Hebrews 12:1-2 (TM)

In other words, keep things simple. Keep your load light. Get rid of what you don't need, and shake off the extra spiritual baggage. One of things I just have no time or tolerance for anymore is suffocating legalism. I have seen the weight of legalism crush and quench many people. For too long the church has put rules and process over relationship. They have valued institutions over compassion, and sometimes practices over God himself. If there was one truth I see throughout scripture, it is that we do in fact serve a mysterious, amazing, sometimes unpredictable God. As much as we want to put God in a box, he is the holy wind who comes and goes as He pleases. Life is just too short to waste time in the debates of legalism and it will certainly kill a strong finish.

When I talk about this passage to the men at Harbor events, I often use an illustration from the movie *The Book of Eli*. The story is set in post-apocalyptic America. Most people have been wiped out by nuclear war. Not much of value is left, and the people who have survived are fighting for anything they can get their hands on. In the middle of this mess, Eli hears a voice that leads him to a book and gives him the mission of taking this book west, until he hits the ocean. He does not know why, but he knows he will be protected. He runs into a ton of obstacles and struggles along the way.

From the very beginning, Eli travels light. He carries only what he needs for the next leg of the journey, which is a good thing because he's being hunted by men who want the book. Eventually the bad guys catch up to him. As the book is taken from him, one guy asks Eli if he believes God is good. Eli responds, "All the time." At that moment the guy shoots him, taunts his faith by asking him where his protection is now, and leaves him to die.

Wow, that took a dark turn, but the story is not over. After the men leave, despite the hits, despite the devastating event that had taken place, despite his questions about why God did not protect him in that moment, despite the shot that nearly took him out, Eli struggles to his feet and continues to head west one slow step at a time. Through almost unbearable and near-fatal circumstance, he continues to trust the voice that has led and protected him to that point. The only way he could make the next leg of his journey, I mean absolutely the only way he could have taken those next steps, was to carry a very light load. Physically, emotionally, and spiritually his load had to be light. No heavy pack weighs him down. He has no extra equipment to carry, no emotional baggage to quell him, no legalism, or empty spirtual cliches. Just a raw, honest faith. One step after another he simply does what the voice told him to do. His mission is simple and clear.

That is a powerful picture of what it takes to not only stay on this spiritual journey, but to finish it well no matter what life throws at you. Like Eli, we must learn to keep the main thing the main thing. The rest will just bog us down. A light load helps us stay flexible when the wind of God blows another direction. A light load allows us to power through those times when we don't think we can take another step. And a light load gives us a much better shot at keeping our

THIN PLACES | BY TIM BOHLKE

heads up so we don't miss the thin places along the way. Sometimes a light load can literally keep us alive.

The older I get the more obvious the message of Hebrews 12 becomes. Life is just too darn short to carry any extra spiritual, physical, or emotional baggage. I want to do my best to lean into the issues that need to be faced then, casting everthing else aside, taking only the most critical things with me on the journey.

THE IMPACT OF THE LOAD

When I was in college I lived in a dorm that was far from where most of my classes met. Because I didn't want to walk back to my room during the day, especially in those cold Nebraska winters, I carried all the books and notebooks I would need in my backpack. Toward the end of the semester, I went to the medical center with shoulder and neck pain. I was playing a lot of sports and figured it was some kind of injury. Eventually we figured out I always carried those books on the same shoulder and it was starting to affect everything. It impacted how I slept, and how I played. It was not until I balanced things out and only took the books I needed at the time, that the pain went away.

We can carry stress, struggle, disappointments, grief, and unforgiveness in our bodies. A gastro intestinal doctor recently told me that eighty percent of his patients do not have a physical medical problem. Their problems are the result of stress. We carry so much that we don't need to—shame, regret, sin, unforgiveness, dreams, expectations, even responsibilities and roles that aren't really ours to own. I used to get into debates over so many different Christian beliefs. There are such sharp disagreements on so many issues. What is absolutely critical to one person, is not important to others. Several years ago, I decided to hold to the basics, to stick to the very central core issues, and let the rest go.

So many of us carry the weight of unforgiveness. It weighs us down, it hardens our hearts, and it can make us bitter. For many of us, there may be sin issues that we need to let go of and move on from, just like the woman Jesus encountered in John 8.

Jesus and the disciples had been busy. The press of ministry had been intense. At the beginning of John 8, they seem to pause. Jesus is sitting down when another confrontation arises. The legalistic religious leaders of the day are tired of this rabbi stirring things up, so they set what they think is a trap.

The scribes and Pharisees brought a woman caught in adultery, and having set her in the center of the court, they said to Him, 'Teacher, this woman has been caught in adultery, in the very act. Now in the Law Moses commanded us to stone such women; What do you say?' ...But Jesus stooped down and with his finger wrote on the ground... He straightened up, and said to them, 'He who is without sin among you, let him be the first to throw the stone at her.' ...When they heard this, they began to go out one by one... Then Jesus turned to the woman and said, 'Go. From now on sin no more.'

John 8:3-11 (NASB)

Can you feel the heavy load that this woman was carrying being lifted off her? Can you imagine how freeing that moment was when she was offered such forgiveness and grace? But what about those accusers, the ones ready to stone her? Can you sense the condemning judgement and rage that weighs them down as they grip those stones so tightly their knuckles turn white? They had been carrying the role of judgments that wasn't theirs to bear. There is an interesting statement in verse 12. "Then one by one they laid down their stones and went out, beginning with the older ones." That is fascinating. It offers perhaps a reflective deeply interactive moment in this story.

Jesus changes everything in a razor thin moment by saying, "He who is without sin cast the first stone." Slowly, one by one, the accusers lighten their own loads, lay down the stones and leave. And why the older ones first? Perhaps because the others were waiting on their lead. Perhaps the weight of judging others and then having to go home and look into the mirror was taking its toll. Perhaps they were just tired of carrying rocks. This story begs us to consider if there is anything we are carrying that we need to loosen our grip on. Is there anything we need to set down?

IT'S ABOUT CONTROL

John 12:25 (TM) says, "In the same way, anyone who holds on to life just as it is destroys that life. But if you let it go, reckless in your love, you'll have it forever, real and eternal." If we hold something too tightly, good or bad, success or failures, disappointments or excitement, we can quench life, suffocate it, and even kill parts of ourselves.

So I often ask myself, what am I holding too tightly? Where do I need to loosen my grip? Is fear driving me to hold or cling to something so tightly that I am restricting some needed growth as a result? The thought that I can control something and dictate the outcome by keeping my grip tight is a fallacy. I know. I've gripped things too tightly, including Dylan's dreams of playing college basketball.

During the summer before his senior year of high school, I needed to get away. This should have been the final summer of travel and tournaments and making memories on the basketball court. Instead, Dylan was sitting at home recovering from another surgery. With my wife's encouragement (I think she maybe needed a break from me), I headed to some favorite places in southern Wyoming and Northern Colorado, hoping somehow God would meet me there.

After a couple of days in Steamboat, and the rush of amazing memories of the times we'd enjoyed with our kids in that place, I could feel my heart start to soften. I had so much to be thankful for. Memories of my kids catching their first trout at Hahns Peak Lake. The numerous elk and bear that we had seen through those years. Quiet nights of games and fun that the five of us shared in front of the fire pit at our cabin. So many simple days packed with memorable moments. My last full day there I went on a long mountain bike ride and began to push myself hard. As I approached a meadow I found a rock where I could rest for a bit. I could feel the rage well up in me. I let out a few yells. I am sure if anyone heard them, they headed the other direction fast.

Then I sat.

And waited.

After a long time of silence, these very clear, very simple words came to me: "Tim, you have to let this go. You must let it go and don't leave this rock until you do. You can't get back on this bike until you're done. I've got this. Let it go."

Everything in me wanted to fix this for Dylan. But I realized then I couldn't. I had traveled to other parts of the world, I had done everything I possibly could and I still could not make it work. I realized I had no choice. It was trust God or get bitter. I could not ultimately control it anyway. I had to let it go.

That was not really what I wanted to hear. I wanted to hear a healing word, I wanted to hear something specific about why all of this was happening to Dylan. I wanted to hear that he was going to get the scholarship after all and play college basketball. I wanted a redemption story. I wanted to get a clear message on what I needed to do to fix the entire situation so I could be rid of the anger and disappointment I felt toward God. But what I heard was, "Let it go."

In that thin place, I started a process of letting go, a process that I am still in the middle of today. On that rock, God began to change my perspective. That moment helped me face the next stretch with greater resilience. Everything did not suddenly become okay, but I will say when I stepped off that rock, I felt like a twenty-pound rock came off my shoulders, and the slow process of healing began. I started to see how far outside my control circumstances really were. I began to admit that there was nothing I could do to make this right. As I sat on that rock I also realized how mad and disappointed I was in myself. Sometimes struggle and pain come to us through our own decisions, but so many times the hurt comes to us by the decisions and the evil of others, and I couldn't stop it. I couldn't always protect my kids in the past, and I knew, in reality, I was very limited in being able to protect them in the future. I had to let that façade of control go as well. Recently, as I was deeply struggling and carrying the weight of the pain of one of our kids, my young son sent me this text. As I read the words of a twenty-three-year-old, I realized he never could have written these words if he had not gone through the intense struggles of his life just a few years earlier.

"Dad, I wanted to remind you of how you have shared what it was like for you to see me go through the pain and suffering during my basketball days. How much of that you put on yourself to get me better, but you just could not do it. Wanted to remind you of your own words to not put this on yourself. For you simply do not have the power to fix this. No doubt you can be used in powerful ways, but this just is not

under your control, which I know is tough for you because as a father you want to protect us and even save us from stuff, but you can't do it. That is the Lords job so you need to let Him take it."

THE WEIGHT OF THE GOOD STUFF

It's been a few years since I sat on that rock in a meadow in Colorado. I left that rock that day aware that I needed to continue to trust God no matter what, even when things don't turn out in the ways that I had so fervently prayed, and even when things make no sense. I'm still in the process of letting go, which brings me back to Hebrews chapter 12. The passage starts by challenging us to cast off everything that hinders. Many of us have tremendous opportunities and choices in this life. We carry the bad, but also so much of the good of our families with us. We carry their successes, dreams, and accomplishments as well as our own. Even that good baggage can get pretty heavy.

Many of us are involved in so many good things, and often we keep adding and adding but never let anything go. So our steps get slower, the pack becomes heavier, and the chance to stay alert to see and experience thin moments is significantly diminished. Can you truly continue to carry everything right now? Do you have enough space in your life to give yourself to the things you are most passionate about, or do those things continue to take a backseat to the urgent things that can crowd our days? Can you continue to carry your current load over the long haul? I have heard it said that giving yourself to a lot of good things keeps you from giving yourself to great things. Often we must let some good things go before we can more clearly focus on the most critical things in our lives and on our calendars.

This passage in Hebrews asks us to slow down and look at everything that we are carrying. If there is something that hinders us, slows us down, blocks our view, confuses us, or diminishes our focus, then shake it loose, cast it off, loosen your grip, and release it. If we are going to experience and enter in to those thin places when they come, first we need to let go.

ALERT

Don't let the moments pass. Don't miss it.

Keep your eyes open. Ready. Expectant. You just never know when those needed thin places will come.

There was a moment when Walter Mitty knew what he had to do. He cast everything aside—his routine, his responsibilities, his inhibitions, and his fears. As he threw off his baggage and began his hero's journey, he was backed by an amazing soundtrack. Don't we all need an amazing soundtrack for our quests? Music that helps connect us to the significant moments on our journey? One of the songs exhorted Walter not to let the moment pass. He realized (no doubt with the help of the lyrics) that the only way he would get where he needed to go was to drop everything, leave his pretend world, and really start living. He could no longer let the moments of each day pass. It was time to move.

This truth that we must not let things pass is so critical to understanding the idea of thin places, to grasping hold of those moments that can change our lives forever.

Our first day in Iceland was one of the most significant of our pilgrimage. What made that day memorable was not our ultimate destination but our ability to slow down, take some detours, make some unplanned stops, and fully embrace the moments along the way.

We were on a surreal road to Vik, a sleepy fishing village in Southern Iceland. It was a long drive, but we'd heard Vik was one place we should visit. We set out and encountered one amazing thing after another. If we had pushed through to Vik too quickly we would have missed stunning waterfalls, which seemed even more amazing in the fog and light rain. We would have driven right past the little farming village where we found the church. We wandered through the cemetery and stories called out to us from the grave stones marking the lives of missionaries and farmers who'd lived hundreds of years before.

At one point on the road to Vik, my son jumped out of the car to kick a ball and was joined by a dog who came out of nowhere and joined him in an impromptu game of soccer. The two of them spent a few minutes playing, my son kicking the ball toward the goal and the dog blocking his best shots. We took an off-road drive up the side of a cliff. When we arrived at the edge, we were looking straight down a vertical face on a beautiful black sand beach that ran along the rugged coastline as far as the eye could see.

We walked to a glacier through black rock and lava dust, reminders of the volcanic eruption a few years before. As I stood in that place of fire and ice, I saw a real picture of life this side of heaven. Moments of light and of darkness, cold and warmth, black and white, and often an insane mix of all of it.

We stumbled upon an old tractor. It was an Allis-Chalmers tractor—the same kind my dad and his dad used on our farm in central Nebraska. It was a piercing reminder of how fast time goes and how small our world really is. My dad, who has been gone for almost thirty years now, has something in common with this farmer on the southern tip of Iceland.

We finally got to Vik about ten that night. If we had arrived any earlier, we would have missed the beauty of the midnight sun. We would have missed the locals settling in for the evening and our crazy chance meeting with another soul from Nebraska who just happened to be in this little pub on a side street in Vik, Iceland at the same moment we were. God must take delight in orchestrating these divine encounters. If we had arrived earlier, we would have missed hiking behind a beautiful waterfall at midnight, the sun still setting, and experiencing a surreal mix of color, temperature, and sites that rarely converge in a single moment. We had this overwhelming feeling that we really were on the edge of the world.

It was one of only a few places on our trip that fully captivated all of us. We wanted to remain in that moment, to just be fully present there. As the sun moved laterally along the sky just under the horizon, I thought of words spoken by Gandalf in The Hobbit:

"There are no safe paths in this part of the world. You are over the Edge of the Wild now...what dangers, unknowns and adventure awaits."

-J.R.R. Tolkien

In that moment behind that waterfall I thought this is what it was supposed to be like! This is a glimpse of Eden! This is what God really intended when He put us on this earth. He intended us to pursue and discover, to explore his mysterious, wild, unpredictable creation that is a reflection of who He is. Our spiritual journeys were never meant to be about passive consumerism, sitting in a pew, and wrestling through lists of duties and obligations. He made us for more! We were designed for the reckless, heart-pounding pursuit on the Edge of the Wild, not a boring routine of dos and don'ts, of lists and shoulds. Faith was meant to be this free, all-in pursuit of God and what He has for us—a journey that holds no guarantees of safety or outcomes this side of heaven, but an invitation to what our desperate souls long for.

I stood behind that waterfall and soaked it all in. Leaving that place about an hour later was tough to do, but that's the way it is with thin place moments. They come, and they pass. We can't hold on to them. If we grip too tightly, the moments just sift through our fingers.

All of that happened on one day. A day when we changed things up. A day when we broke from the plan. We listened. We watched and we took some turns that were not on the map. We did our best in that day to slow down and remain alert to anything that might come our way.

We need to approach each day with that same kind of heightened alertness. We can't allow ourselves to get too settled in, to be so caught up in the day-to-day routine that we miss the important stuff. Sometimes the moments that change everything occur on ordinary days. Think about Moses and that radical encounter with God at the burning bush.

It was a day like so many other days in the forty years Moses had been shepherding sheep and working his father-in-law's business in the desert. He had the routine down. Take the sheep into the desert to find food, protect them, watch over them, and bring them back to a place of safety. The scenery, the sheep, the thoughts, the job itself had to have been very much the same every day of the four decades that Moses had been faithfully doing his job. Moses, who at the time was close to eighty years old, had to be thinking, "This is life. This is how I'm going to finish this out." And it was probably a pretty good, easy, comfortable, safe life.

But this was Moses. His mom gave him up and put him in a basket in the Nile River to protect him from Pharaoh who was killing off Hebrew boys to control the population. Through circumstances that could only happen by God's hand, Moses was taken out of the river and into Pharaoh's family. He lived a life of privilege, power, and endless opportunity. But as an adult, he discovered who he really was—the son of Hebrew slaves— and things changed quickly. He became tuned in to the struggle of his people who were under the weight of slavery. He could no longer ignore what went on around him. He was much more alert. One day, he saw the cruelty of an Egyptian toward one of the Hebrews and Moses snapped. He killed the Egyptian. As a result, he was banished forever into the desert wilderness. And forty years later, Moses was an older man, likely settled in and ready to ride out what days he had left...until that day that was different than the previous 14,400 days in the dessert...

THE MOST FAMOUS ENCOUNTER BETWEEN GOD AND MOSES

Now Moses was pasturing the flock of Jethro his father-in-law, the priest of Midian; and he led the flock to the west side of the wilderness and came to Horeb, the mountain of God. The angel of the Lord appeared to him in a blazing fire from the midst of a bush; and he looked, and behold, the bush was burning with fire, yet the bush was not consumed. So Moses said, 'I must turn aside now and see this marvelous sight, why the bush is not burned up.' When the Lord saw that he turned aside to look, God called to him from the midst of the bush and said, 'Moses, Moses!' And he said, 'Here I am.' Then He said, 'Do not come near here; remove your sandals from your feet, for the place on which you are standing is holy ground.' He said also, 'I am the God of your father, the God of Abraham, the God of Isaac, and the God of Jacob.' Then Moses hid his face, for he was afraid to look at God.

The Lord said, 'I have surely seen the affliction of My people who are in Egypt, and have given heed to their cry because of their taskmasters, for I am aware of their sufferings. So I have come down to deliver them from the power of the Egyptians, and to bring them up from that land to a good and spacious land, to a land flowing with milk and honey, to the place of the Canaanite and the Hittite and the Amorite and the Perizzite and the Hivite and the Jebusite. Now, behold, the cry of the sons of Israel has come to Me; furthermore, I have seen the oppression with which the Egyptians are oppressing them.

Therefore, come now, and I will send you to Pharaoh, so that you may bring My people, the sons of Israel, out of Egypt.'

Exodus 3:1-10 (NASB)

Many things stand out from this passage, and it's important that we don't miss them.

First, God is speaking. Clearly this is an out-of-the-ordinary moment, an amazing thin place. God, for whatever His reasons, decides to show up and have an audible conversation with Moses. This doesn't happen every day. In fact, it had not happened to Moses in the forty years he'd been in the desert.

The other significant part of this story is that Moses was ready and willing to step into that moment. He was alert. He didn't miss it! Slow down for a moment and read verse 4. "When Moses saw the bush burning he said, 'I must turn aside now and see this marvelous sight, why the bush is not burned up.' When the Lord saw that he turned aside to look, God called to him from the midst of the bush."

Now think about that. When God saw that Moses turned, then He spoke. The calling— the trajectory of Moses, his family, and the world changed because Moses turned aside. It raises a few questions, doesn't it?

Was God really waiting on Moses to turn aside and look?

What was it about this day that caused Moses to turn toward God's presence?

Could that bush have been burning all along? Did Moses take a different path down the mountain this time?

Was he nudged to take that route that day?

And the big one: Why not sooner? It had been forty years since Moses had been banished from Egypt. *Forty years.* And during those years, the Hebrews were being crushed by the weight of slavery. People were suffering and dying. Why did God wait so long?

We can get lost in such questions, and there are plenty of them. They are important to ask, but we can't allow them to cause us to miss some critical points we need to hear:

- God showed up in a very thin place.

- Moses was alert. He was ready to listen.

- God waited for Moses to turn before He spoke.

I wonder what we have missed because we failed to slow down. Have there been times when God was waiting for us to turn aside and look? Has the pace, and even our addiction to a busy lifestyle, robbed us of those moments? There have been so many times that I failed to stop, pause, look, and listen, so many times I wished I would have taken time to soak in the moment. It's hard to list what I may have missed, but I do know what I've experienced in some of those simple moments when I did turn aside.

During a family trip to Hawaii a few years ago we were on a quest to the north shore on Oahu. Snorkeling, waterfalls, cliffs, and rock jumping into the ocean were on the agenda. On the drive, I noticed a few cars pulled over on the side of the road. I decided to check it out.

I got the eye rolls. The crew was tired of me pulling over for all the sights. They wanted to keep moving and get to the destination. I couldn't get anyone to get out of that car so I went to the beach alone. What I got to see was amazing. Giant sea turtles making their way up the beach. It was quite a sight seeing these ancient-looking creatures emerge from the surf and come on to land. It took ten minutes and those who remained in the car missed it.

Another moment I nearly missed was one of my son's AAU basketball tournaments in St. Louis the summer before his junior year in high school. In spite of the deep disappointment of all his injuries and missed opportunities, some of the best fun I've had was watching him play in those summer tournaments. This summer was a particularly great one. He'd been playing well and college recruiting was accelerating. We'd already been to a few tourneys that summer and had a family wedding I needed to attend. As the time for me to leave for the wedding came close, I was struggling. I didn't want to miss this tournament. I reminded myself that I very seldom missed games, and that it was important to my extended family and my niece that I not miss the wedding.

I started the drive home, but an hour in I just couldn't shake the feeling. I turned around and headed back to St. Louis to watch this last tournament of the summer. Dylan had the best tournament of his life against great competition. He led his team on several comebacks, and some near comebacks. What I didn't know at the time was that would be the last summer tournament he would ever play. I thought I would have another summer full of games, but the following summer was full of physical therapy, surgeries, and rehab.

In our culture, it's so easy to keep moving, keep running, keep pressing. We move from one thing to the next without thinking or listening to our intuition, and maybe miss the burning bush in our own backyard. Let's go back to the story of Moses and look a little deeper. Let's not move too fast and rush past what God might be wanting us to see, hear, and experience.

Part of why Moses encountered a thin place on that day had to be that he was ready. He was attentive. Alert. We can see that in his actions. He paused. He stopped. He listened. Maybe for the first time in his life he was ready. He also recognized the moment was different. It was significant. It was weighty. He was on holy ground.

Let's look more closely at God's part. He spoke clearly, but He did not give Moses a lot of facts, statistics, or specific plans. All He really said was, "Hey, Moses. I'm sending you to Pharaoh and I'll be with you." Moses had to step out. He had to be willing to be the one guy to go to the most powerful country on earth and lead a million people out of slavery. If God had laid out all of the details and given Moses a clue about what was ahead of him, would the outcome of this encounter have been different? It seems to me that in that thin place, God gave Moses exactly what he needed for the moment.

I also notice that what God asked Moses to do in that thin place was consistent with Moses' passion, history, and life experiences. I doubt there was anyone on earth better equipped to go to Egypt and confront Pharaoh. Moses' journey made him the perfect guy for the job. Maybe it took forty years in the desert before he was ready for this assignment.

I thought about this story often as we launched Harbor. My experience, failures and success, my passions, strengths, and talents, and ultimately God's calling, made me the right person to step out and help create an unconventional leadership journey. But I had to be alert. I had to be willing. I had to trust that even though I didn't know all the details, God was with me.

Thin place moments, as author Ruth Haley Barton notes, "awaken us to extraordinary in the ordinary." But I fear our senses are dulled. We are numb. So much is vying for our attention that we may miss those moments when God is begging us to turn aside. So how can we remain alert? I don't have an easy three-step process that works for everyone, but I can share some things from my own life that have helped me stay alert.

REMEMBER

This one is so vital I've included an entire chapter on the topic. We must remember the ways God has shown up in the past. This again would be a good time to put down this book, pick up a journal, and record those moments, those times, those seasons when God uniquely met you. Write them down. Who were you with? Where were you? What were you doing? Was it as simple as a sunset, like I experienced in Estes Park a few years ago? Was it through pain, struggle or trauma? Capture the thoughts that come to mind.

CULTIVATE THE SKILL OF BEING ATTENTIVE

When my oldest son was a toddler, if he sensed we were not listening to him, he used to grab our faces and make us look at him. Even at two he knew we were going to miss something important if we were not present with him in that moment.

This can be a hard thing, especially for us guys. My wife often tells me that when I arrive home at the end of day, I'm often not fully present. This practice of being attentive is flat out hard work, but slowing down helps me. Creating gaps, taking space, taking a few deep breaths, going for a bike ride in the middle of the day, or forcing myself to just sit quietly for a few minutes all help to quiet my mind and allow me to focus on the present.

CHANGE IT UP

Do things differently. Take a new route home from work. Look a little closer when things happen. Ask that extra question. Break the routine. Read a different translation of the Bible. Put the Bible down and go for a hike or ride instead. Shake yourself out of business as usual. Refuse to just settle in and coast.

A few years back we took some of the Rhythm in Twenty guys on a pretty epic hike. It was the last day of a three-year journey with these leaders from around the country. We took the whole group up to about twelve-thousand feet on a peak that has a great view of the valley above Crested Butte, Colorado. It was an amazing day and those of us that made it to the summit soaked in the moment. Several others were still struggling to make the last stretch of what was a pretty aggressive hike. A few guys wanted to keep moving, and press forward to make the next peak. One of our leaders, Mike, normally would have been in that group itching to take on the next challenge. He's a CrossFit guy and native Coloradoan who has hiked many peaks. But this time he decided to stay, to soak in the views and to encourage those who were still struggling up the side of that mountain. Because he stayed back, he got to see the last few guys reach that first summit. His words, his encouragement, and ultimately his hand pulled those guys up those last few feet. He shared some incredible moments with guys that he would have missed had he pressed on and simply done what came easily and naturally for him. That day he did something a bit out of character and was able to participate in a thin place moment with some leaders who needed him. And what he did not fully realize at the time was he needed to slow down, wait, and fully be in that moment.

SCHEDULE IT

Schedule some gaps in your calendar, some extended time of solitude in the next month. Not next quarter or next year but in the next thirty days. Start to practice this idea of listening, waiting, attending, and staying alert. It's hard at first but stay with it. Learn to wait. Train yourself to listen.

My sons and I are big fans of the Chicago Cubs, not lifers, like some, but more than bandwagon fans. I've been going to Wrigley field since college and it is always an amazing experience. These last couple of years have been fun as the team acquired amazing talent and got better and better. One of their young infielders, Addison Russel, is known for making amazing plays. After Russel robbed an opposing batter of a sure base hit, manager Joe Madden said, "He just willed his glove on that ball at the end of it. That would be just anticipation, being in the moment, just totally being focused, not worrying about an at bat, or anything else that happened over the last twenty-four hours. He was just in the moment, and that was what permitted him to make that play."

Being in the moment allows us to make the play. It sounds so simple, but we know it's not. To be in the moment, we must fully embrace who we are and what we are about. We must refuse to get stuck in the past or the future. We must be disciplined, intentional, and anticipative.

THIN PLACES WITH OTHERS

While I've been talking mostly about remaining alert so we don't miss the thin places in relationship with God, we must also be alert to the times we need to turn aside and experience the hearts of those closest to us. Many of us have experienced moments when pretense, posing, and expectations fall away as we catch a glimpse of the soul of our spouse, or our child, or even the co-conspirators who lead alongside us.

Several years ago, when Dylan was in elementary school, I was living life at a frantic pace. Finding a rhythm to my life had been a struggle. I was having a hard time just keeping up with what was in front of me. Out of nowhere a friend called and offered me tickets for an NBA playoff game between the Lakers and Nuggets in Denver. I love basketball. I love watching it and playing it, but then-eleven-year-old Dylan loved it more. The Lakers have been his team since.... well since birth. There was one problem. Typically, I would stretch an experience out but I couldn't do it this time. The only way I could pull it off was to drive the fifteen hours up and back on the same day, driving virtually all night on the way home. Many people called me crazy, but we decided to go for it.

It was a great day! Waiting by the Lakers' hotel so Dylan could crawl up a lamp post just to catch a glimpse of Kobe Bryant and then watching him light up when the Lakers took the floor made it totally worth it. This spontaneous trip, this turning aside to seize a moment with my son, was about so more than a basketball game: it was about making time, making family a priority, and just having fun. One of the great challenges in life and leadership is to turn aside from the noise and busyness for these moments so we don't miss the hearts of those closest to us.

Now Dylan has graduated from college, and I'm glad I didn't miss that chance and the many others since then to be present as best I could. Just over a year ago we took a similar trip to see Kobe's last road game before his retirement. We jumped into the car and drove fourteen hours for a three-hour game in Oklahoma City. As we waited near the court for the Lakers to take the court, and many times throughout that game, Dylan had that same smile, the same look of anticipation, excitement, and thankfulness that he'd had years before as a young boy. That drive was so worth it.

Or there are those moments you just need to go fishing. I learned that from my dad. He was a farmer and the summers were some of the busiest work times. But when I was little he told me that whenever it rained an inch we could go fishing. And he always followed through. Even if there was a ton of work to be done, we would still grab our fishing poles and head out. I picked up some great life lessons there. Sometimes making time and staying alert is spontaneous and happens in the moment. Sometimes it takes planning.

Recently it took some time with my oldest son Drew, good friends, and a road trip to South Dakota to get me to totally disconnect. It was just three days but they were filled with great stories and unique moments like the rodeo-riding, car mechanic waitress who told us we'd better keep our rooms clean or she would kick our butts. She was the hotel maid as well! Or the classic fishing moments when one of the fishing guides took my friend and his son to another spot because they weren't catching anything. Two minutes after they left, we started catching one walleye after another.

It didn't take much; just a little planning and a willingness to hit the road. And God met me there. He met me right in the middle of doing the things I love most—sharing unique experiences, family, friends, travel, lots of laughs, and some fishing. Thanks to that trip, I feel much better prepared for the busy season ahead of me. Sometimes you have to find a way to really change things up, get out of the routine, and go.

Don't miss it! Don't let the moments pass!

It may take some adjustments, maybe some extra resources, and even some personal sacrifice for us to step off the treadmill and be engaged in the present, but it is so worth it. It's worth it every single time. Plan a trip, make a memory with someone close to you. Whatever you love to do, take time to get away and enjoy it. Slow down this crazy pace you keep and hang out the "gone fishing" sign once in a while. Those times will help fill your tank and make it so much easier to stay alert and ready for whatever God has in store.

As we wind up this discussion of staying alert, I think about a verse in Habakkuk 2. This prophet implores us to stay at our guard post, alert and ready to hear from God. Then he tells us to write down what God says so we can read it on the run.

I'll climb to the lookout tower and scan the horizon.
I'll wait to see what God says...

And then God answered: "Write this.
  Write what you see.
Write it out in big block letters
  so that it can be read on the run.
This vision-message is a witness
  pointing to what's coming.

It aches for the coming—it can hardly wait!

And it doesn't lie.

If it seems slow in coming, wait.

It's on its way. It will come right on time.

Habakkuk 2:1-3 (TM)

Being ready and alert means being there for the long haul, unwavering, not thrown off course, not falling asleep at our post. Are you alert and ready to turn aside and embrace those burning bush moments along the road to Vik, or wherever the Wild Goose leads in your own journey?

AWAKEN

Wake up sleeper, rise from the dead and Christ will shine
a light on you.

Ephesians 5:14 (NIV)

It's not hard to stay awake in Iceland in the summer. Coming from the states, we were wide awake when others back home were sleeping, which was perfect because some of the most amazing times happened when we typically would have been in bed. Late evening through midnight is the best times to see the sights. No one is on the roads and it felt like we had the sights and sounds of Iceland all to ourselves. One night we ventured to an incredible three-tiered inland waterfall and we were nearly the only ones there. As it neared midnight and sunset and that sun glided across the horizon, we experienced a surreal mix of sights and colors across the open fields, the steam from the geysers rolling through the valleys, the mist coming off the massive waterfalls that was inviting and mysterious.

We felt terrifically alive, and that was a theme at many of the waterfalls we encountered in Iceland. Through glaciers, cliffs, lava, and black beaches, we experienced a deeper awareness of God and who He is. But there was something about the waterfalls. Their presence did not beg for attention, yet we were totally compelled by them and simply had to engage them. Gulfoss is a multi-tiered waterfall whose last section falls deeply into the abyss. It's a stop-you-in-your tracks reminder of the deeply mysterious, unsafe and unpredictable aspects of God.

We stood under Skogofass, a monster fall of sheer power, absorbed by the cold and wet, the dark grays and mist, and a rush of adrenaline. It was an invitation of sorts, a beckoning from an almost-audible voice that said, "Enter this journey if you dare. No guarantees. No safeguards. No noticeable boundaries or fences... but if you want to really feel alive, then enter..."

In contrast, we were overcome by the quiet beauty of Seljalandsfoss. Standing behind this cascading waterfall in the midnight light, a deafening silence invited us to linger and enjoy the moment. Iceland's waterfalls cry out to the reality that God is untamed, wild, adventurous, beautiful, awe-inspiring, deeply quiet, reflective, and mysterious.

We experienced those unique, late night moments, because we were awake. Literally. Being fully awake physically and spiritually at the opportune moment gave us a chance to see and experience something others will certainly miss.

When we launched Harbor Ministries, one of my hopes was to wake up leaders who were coasting, who were settling, or backing away from dangerous pursuits. When the faith of a leader loses its edge, when we doze off and get bored, or forget what it was like to take risks and pursue this mysterious God and all He has for us, everyone loses. We lose. Our families lose, and those we lead lose. So we wanted to think outside the box. What we discovered was we had to blow up the box to create the space and pace necessary for leadership events that would make a difference over the long haul. It would take something new to awaken leaders—wake up their senses and emotions, and engage them in the kind of deep, authentic relationship God wants with each of us. We had to be open to the Wild Goose and the variety of ways He might choose to engage the hearts of leaders and help them reconnect with the dangerous journey they were once on.

As the Rhythm and Rogue journeys began to unfold, we found ourselves consistently gravitating to the song "Awake my Soul" by Mumford and Sons, This song represented much of what we were seeking. The lyrics alone embraced so much of what we hoped for the leaders as they came into Harbor events. We longed to see God use these leadership journeys to re-awaken something deep within them—to re-ignite that passionate, all-in, all-out pursuit of God that makes leaders dangerous in the first place.

You need to listen to that song. Seriously. Put down this book, buy the song on iTunes, and crank it. With the right mindset, it may be some of the best worship you will experience. Sit with it. Listen to it again, and ask yourself if you really believe the words at the end: Awake my soul... awake my soul... We were made to meet our maker...

That is what we were made for. That is how we were designed. We were made to experience God in random and intentional moments, in the mundane and the extraordinary, each of us in our own unique, crazy, amazing way.

My wife and I meet God in different ways. Our pathways to God and what ignites and stirs our souls are not the same. This makes finding a church interesting. For me the music, the place, the environment, and the overall experience are really important. For her, intellectual challenge and depth of teaching are critical. Whatever our path, we need to identify it, name it, and pursue it. Some find those thin place moments with God through reading, study, and contemplation; others through service and action. Some people encounter God through various forms of art, others through solitude. Some through crowds of people, others through nature and the sheer beauty of creation. For people like Matt, God shows up in music.

Matt came to the very first Rhythm in Twenty event. He was leading in a large, influential church. In so many he ways was serving right in his sweet spot, but he was also carrying a lot of emotional weight. He had walked through a ton of loss with others, and had lost a close friend himself. He arrived at Harbor needing to hear from God, needing to have his heart awakened so he could be ready for the season ahead. Matt needed to experience God in a fresh way. He needed to be reminded that he was made to meet his maker. So he entered a three-year Rhythm in Twenty journey with nineteen other guys. Through the next couple of years, God met each of those leaders in unique ways. He woke them up and reconnected them to the things that were life-giving, engaged their souls, and filled our emotional and spiritual tanks.

Matt didn't wake up because of worship, times of solitude, the Bible, or prayer, at least not in their conventional forms. Music shook his soul alive. Not just any music, but his favorite group, Over the Rhine. Music was something that had taken him to a deeper place—a better place—in the past, so Matt became more intentional about listening to Over the Rhine and going to their concerts.

He found that gave him the bolt of energy and passion he needed to continue the fight.

What awakens my soul are times of solitude, encounters with nature, and music, especially when I attend concerts with friends or family. In concerts featuring U2, Mumford and Sons, Tom Petty, and The Lumineers, I have experienced God in deep ways I would not have expected. Those are great reminders that God can create thin places anywhere, in any context He chooses.

Random bike rides also stir my soul. In spring and summer, I always have my bike strapped on the back on my car. Any time I have a spare hour I will head to the trail. It's refreshing and gives me a surge of energy I often need. It quiets me down and gives me a sense that things will be okay. No wonder I grieve when those Nebraska winters settle in.

For the past decade, I've made it a habit to set aside one day each month for silence and solitude, for time to just quiet down and listen. Most of the time I hear nothing, yet I almost always come away more at peace, more centered, and with a sense that I can navigate the stormy seas of leadership. I need these days to keep myself and my spiritual journey fresh, alive, and moving.

The men who come into our leadership journeys know they are there for a purpose. They know that God has created a restless stir that caused them to fly across the country to join others they do not know, to listen, and to process life with leaders they have never heard of. You can see it in their eyes. They arrive with a mix of excitement and, "Oh crap! What have I got myself into?" But they come. They show up. As we gather for that first time of connection, we challenge them to see this Harbor experience as holy ground. We invite them into a journey that will require them to be all in for the next few days. Only when they are fully present, not distracted, but alert and awake, are they ready for the thin moments that will surely come.

Caleb was a man whose soul was awake. We find his story in Numbers 13 and 14. God had freed the Israelites from slavery in Egypt. He had parted the Red Sea. He was present with them in a pillar of fire. He provided food and water. They had seen God come through for them again and again. Yet, not all of them were awake.

This nation of hundreds of thousands stands on the edge of the Promised Land, the land that God had told them would be theirs. But they hesitate. They had heard rumors that land was inhabited by great giants and fortified cities that were impossible to breech. So Moses selected twelve leaders to go and spy on the land and bring back a report. Now keep in mind these were the key leaders among hundreds of thousands of people. These were the best of the best, leaders who had seen God show up time and time again. They were there when God reigned down the plagues on Egypt. They were there when, after hundreds of years of slavery, the Hebrew people were freed. They stood beside the Red Sea as God parted those waters. This group of twelve included Joshua and Caleb.

For forty days, these spies explored the Promised Land. They saw clusters of grapes so big that two men had to carry them. They came back and reported that the land flowed with milk and honey, which probably sounded pretty good to people whose main diet was manna. But... the spies also reported that there were indeed large, fortified cities guarded by huge men. Some of the spies described them as giants and the Israelites as mere grasshoppers.

Giants vs. grasshoppers.

It is amazing what happens when we take God out of the equation. When fear, worry, and anxiety set in, we can totally lose perspective and lose sight of what we know to be true.

You can guess how the crowd reacted to this news.

Then Caleb stepped forward.

> *Then Caleb quieted the people before Moses and said, 'We should*
> *by all means go up and take possession of it, for we will surely overcome*
> *it.' But the men who had gone up with him said, 'We are not able to go*
> *up against the people, for they are too strong for us.' So they gave out*
> *to the sons of Israel a bad report of the land which they had spied out,*
> *saying, 'The land through which we have gone, in spying it out, is a land*
> *that devours its inhabitants; and all the people whom we saw in it are*
> *men of great size. There also we saw the Nephilim (the sons of Anak*
> *are part of the Nephilim); and we became like grasshoppers in our own*
> *sight, and so we were in their sight.'*
>
> Numbers 13:30-33 (NASB)

The people missed the moment. When God asked them to trust and risk,
they rebelled in fear. The result? They spent forty years in the wilderness,
enough time for the generation who had witnessed God's miracles during the
exodus to die. Those people did not get to enter God's Promised Land. With two
exceptions: Joshua and Caleb.

> *So the Lord said, 'I have pardoned them according to your word;*
> *but indeed, as I live, all the earth will be filled with the glory of the*
> *Lord. Surely all the men who have seen My glory and My signs which*
> *I performed in Egypt and in the wilderness, yet have put Me to the test*
> *these ten times and have not listened to My voice, shall by no means*

see the land which I swore to their fathers, nor shall any of those who
spurned Me see it...

But...

My servant Caleb, because he has had a different spirit and has
followed Me fully, I will bring into the land which he entered, and his
descendants shall take possession of it.

Exodus 14:20-24 (NASB)

What was it that helped Caleb live a different story? What allowed him to seize the moment? What distinguished Caleb and Joshua from the other great leaders of the day?

First, they remembered. You can sense it in their words and how they reported what they saw in the Promised Land. They remembered the stories of their fathers. They remembered how God had delivered them and the many thin moments on their journey out of Egypt. They remembered the Red Sea. They remembered the pillar of fire that kept the Egyptian army at bay. They remembered the provisions of food and water. In short, they remembered that God has always come through. To be awake, we must remember not to forget the things God has done in the past.

Second, Caleb acted. He had no guarantees, but he put his trust in God and was ready to move forward in faith.

If God is pleased with us, he will lead us into that land, a land that
flows, as they say, with milk and honey. And he'll give it to us. Just don't
rebel against GOD! And don't be afraid of those people. Why, we'll have

them for lunch! They have no protection and God is on our side. Don't
be afraid of them.

Numbers 14:8-10 (TM)

Notice that Caleb did not say there would not be loss, sacrifice, or struggle in taking the land, but that he would rather risk the struggle than cower and fear and rebel against God.

Third, Caleb passionately pursued God. Numbers 13:24 tells us that he followed God fully. He was passionate about God and what he had promised the people. He was ready to act no matter what. He went all in. His hold-nothing-back approach and reckless trust in God distinguished him from the other spies. He was awake and ready when God said, "Trust me."

That reminds me of a scene out of the movie *The Perfect Storm*, which tells the story of the fishing vessel Andrea Gail that I mentioned at the start of this book. Three passengers have been lost at sea in the middle of a colossal collision of a hurricane coming from the south and a Nor'easter bearing down from the north. The Coast Guard has located this tiny vessel at night and a helicopter has flown to the area. Facing darkness and forty-foot waves below, without hesitation the rescuers jumped out of the helicopter. That took training and discipline. That also took passion. It took a passionate connection to the mission they had been trained for. This was their moment.

Now I suspect we all want to be like those rescuers and like Caleb. We want to be the one who trusts even when the odds are stacked against us. We want to be awake and see God beyond and through our circumstances. We want to be the ones who move ahead even when it's more comfortable to stay where we are. We want to be awake to the direction of God when it comes.

A while back I woke up in the middle of the night with the story of Samuel on my mind. I'm not sure why. Maybe God was reminding me how important it is to be awake. I mean, if we want to hear Him, we really need to be awake. In that sleepless night, I read an article about the distant whispers of God. Why, I wondered, does God whisper? Why doesn't He speak to us loudly and clearly? Why is His voice so often quiet and subtle? In Samuel's first thin place encounter with God, God whispered. He whispered to Samuel two or three times during the night and Samuel did not recognize His voice. Samuel needed his mentor Eli to tell him to stay awake, quiet down, and listen to the voice of God. We need someone like Eli in our lives. We need that person in our corner reminding us to stay awake, quiet down, and to listen; that more seasoned ear to remind us that God still speaks, even if in a whisper.

I have an idea about why God might choose to whisper. Our culture is:

Loud.

Busy.

Noisy.

In a world where thousands of messages scream for our attention every single day, a whisper stands out. Perhaps God chooses to whisper so His voice will be:

Different.

Distinguishable.

Unique.

A few times in my life, God's voice has been clear. In those moments, there was a weightiness in the whisper. I recognized it and I long to hear it more often. Can you think of a time when He whispered to you? A time when there was a difference in His voice that caused you to pause and really listen?

A few years ago, I was in Colorado beside a pounding waterfall on the Oh Be Joyful trail near Crested Butte when God really woke me. This rush of ideas and thoughts came so fast I couldn't write them all down. Life came into focus and my future suddenly had some clarity. And it started with a simple question: What do I want in this next season of life to be about? If others were to read my story after the next few years, what would I want them to see and experience?

I had pondered many ways to answer those questions before, but the ideas were vague and hard to hang on to. That day the words came from a deep place, and they came with the speed of the water that was tumbling down that waterfall. And I knew. I knew:

- I want to keep seeking out beautiful places like this. I want to take them in; to be still and really soak in those moments.
- I want to fight for, cheer-lead, and encourage my wife and my kids to chase their dreams.
- I want to fight for the dreams of others, and help them take the steps they need.
- I want whatever years I have left to count. I want them to matter. I want to make a difference.
- I want to inspire others to be quiet, to listen, and to keep chasing the Wild Goose.
- I want adventure and challenge, and friends to seek those out with.
- I don't want to settle.
- I want to laugh, to travel, and somehow to write and capture the crazy thoughts God seems to give me, and hope those words can encourage others.
- I don't want to get stuck in disappointments and struggle.
- I want to take steps that seem impossible.

To hear these things, I need the right posture. I need to be in a place where I am awake but my soul is quiet and undistracted. I need to be alert and remember what it's like to hear God's whisper and to turn aside when He calls.

As I stood on the plains in Iceland replaying the journey that had brought us to the cliff, my mind drifted to the movie *Chasing Mavericks*. This under-the-radar movie tells the true story of Jay Moriarty, a guy with a deep connection with the ocean and an amazing gift for surfing. His passion was to chase the biggest, baddest waves off the coast of Southern California, waves called mavericks. In the movie he asked a friend, "Have you ever seen something and when you saw, you just knew that is what you were put on this earth to do?"

Jay Moriarty trained. He studied, he waited, he dreamed, and then one day he became a legend when he took the risk and rode a monster wave all the way in. Jay's passion was so apparent in the film. You can tell that he was never more alive, never more awake than when he's taking the drop and riding those waves. At the end of movie in a clip of the real Jay talking about life, he says, "You just have to appreciate everything. That's one of the most important things in life, because we only get to do this once, and it's not for a long time, so enjoy it!"

Dylan has been a bit of a maverick chaser. His "maverick" was to play Division 1 basketball. But as you have heard through his story, sometimes you put yourself out there, you take the steps you feel God has led you to take, you take a risk, you follow your passion, and the wave flat out slams you into the beach.

So where are you in the chase? Have the waves slammed you to the bottom or are you riding it in? Is it time to look for another wave? My maverick chaser is pretty discouraged right now... but I have no doubt he will soon be looking for another wave. I believe that even with the risks, even with the disappointment, he knows he was made to live a bigger story. In his heart, I believe he knows he was meant to chase mavericks. All of us are.

As I close out this section on how to pursue thin places, I return to our friend Walter Mitty. Walter was a dreamer, and I really like dreamers, and I love men and women who ask, "Why not?" instead of, "Why?" The problem with Walter was that was all he did. For years he lived in a dream phase. He never stepped out. He didn't have adventures. He never actually chased anything, or experienced life. He just daydreamed.

Like many of us, Walter needed to be shaken. His world needed to be turned upside down to wake him out of his slumber. When he finally took some risks that broke him out of his comfort zone, a spark came back into his eyes. He found wind in his sails and energy in his step. His perspective, attitude, emotions, and the trajectory of his life all changed.

Walter woke up.

Throughout the movie, we're led to believe Sean O'Connell, the rugged, rogue photographer is the hero. You think this is his story. He lived a life of unpredictable, exotic moments, and is famous for his ability to capture those moments on film. Yet, in the end, the real hero is Walter, the regular guy whose mundane job is mocked by others. In the end, it's his loyalty, his faithfulness, the excellence with which he does his job, and his decision to finally take risks that are celebrated. He has become not only a brave man, but a much more complete man.

Walter's challenge was not to just do his job and live out his life as best he could. His challenge was to live a life with a sense of awe and mystery, and to be willing to take risks and seek adventure within the essence of who he was and what he was created to do. I walked away from that movie not wanting to let myself get stuck in a rut, to not bury my desires, talents, or passion. I felt compelled to bring my unique gifts right into the day-to-day realities of my life, to re-connect with desires, to soak in the moments, and to connect deeply with people around me. I wanted to wake up and not settle for daydreaming. Now that is a lot to get from a movie.

I continue to discover what it looks like for me to embrace the realities of my life while remaining determined not to settle. Living with a sense of discovery, welcoming mystery and being willing to take risks—not recklessly, but not living in fear.

Learning to be faithful and true in the day-to-day realities of life while chasing the Wild Goose, that is the challenge. And that may be a heroic way to live. That is living life with our eyes, ears, and souls fully awake and ready.

PART THREE  THE ARRIVAL

THIN MOMENTS

"The history of early Celtic 'saints' and their role in spreading Christianity along the western seaboard as they sought seclusion is well-established. What my work has done is to demonstrate that they could have travelled far further, as far as Iceland, in their quest for the wild places in which to follow their religious life."

-Dr. Kristján Ahronson

For so long, thinking about God as wild, mysterious, and unpredictable was a threat. It did not feel safe for me or for others close to me. It didn't fit some of the theology I had bought into, that a sovereign God has everything planned out, the order was set, and what was going to happen was going to happen no matter what.

It's easier to settle into that line of thinking. It's safe. Now it is true we have a sovereign God who is in control. This world is in His hands and I am so thankful for that... BUT there is also the truth that we absolutely have a wild, adventurous, mysterious, and unpredictable God. I have looked at that truth through many stories throughout this project. Perhaps there is no place in the scripture where this truth is more evident than in the actions of Jesus just a week before the end of his life. Here came Jesus into Jerusalem where he was welcomed as a hero, a conqueror, a deliverer, a king, but He was not going to be the kind of king and conqueror the people hoped for. As he rode into Jerusalem, his first order of business was to go right to the heart of what had become a distracted, unfocused, hypocritical faith for the Hebrew people and leaders. With only a week left in his life on earth, with the clock ticking, this fierce, compassionate, and relentless Wild Goose went to the literal symbolic heart of the Hebrew people. He went to the temple.

> *Jesus went straight to the Temple and threw out everyone who had set up shop, buying and selling. He kicked over the tables of loan sharks and the stalls of dove merchants. He quoted this text: 'My house was designated a house of prayer;*
> *You have made it a hangout for thieves...'*
> *Now there was room for the blind and crippled to get in. They came to Jesus and he healed them.*
>
> Matthew 21:12-17 (TM)

This was not the Jesus I grew up learning about. I was not acquainted with this kind of fierce, intentional, righteous anger. There are many who have studied this text and know much more about the culture than I do. John Eldredge refers to Jesus' actions as "an all-out, sustained assault." He basically started a riot to clear out what, for generations, had been holy ground and sacred space. He did whatever it took to show people that this place had badly lost its way, and if a radical intervention was necessary to illustrate His point, so be it. Even Jesus had to fight to create sacred space.

It was not until the temple was cleared that real ministry could take place. The Message says, "Now there was room for the blind and crippled to get in. They came to Jesus and he healed them." But that didn't happen until the wild and holy God cleared that sacred space, and claimed it for what it was meant to be. This is such a powerful reminder that life is just too short. We cannot afford to waste one day. Get yourself in a place, a holy place. Do whatever you must to clear some space in your own life. Shut off the noise and listen. And don't let yourself forget that you were not intended for safety... for comfort... for just settling in. You were designed for adventure... beauty...risk... and a pursuit of thin places.

So let's get practical for a minute. With this passage from Matthew in mind,

Clear some space.

Physically clear out some space. Clear out a drawer, a closet, a car, or a room, and see how that feels. Then read Matthew 21:12-17 and Mark 11:15-17, and ask yourself what you think of what Jesus did. How does it make you feel to know this action was part of who Jesus was? Does it make you feel comforted? Unsafe? Unsettled? Take a moment to journal your thoughts.

Enter the quiet.

Find a quiet place for fifteen minutes of silence. Turn off the noise, unplug, and just be in the presence of God.

Remember. Recall those times, those seasons, when God broke through in your life. Read Psalm 77 and reflect on the power of remembering. This won't work unless you write these down. If you don't have a journal consider getting one. Or write down some of what comes to mind here in the back of this book. Don't forget.

Clear the sight lines.

It is easier to see, hear, and experience those thin places when they come if we can clear away the emotional and spiritual clutter. There simply is no time for legalism, no time to get locked up in anything that, in the end, really just doesn't matter. Is there anything in your emotional, physical, or spiritual journey that you need to release, surrender, or clear out so that you can see God more clearly?

Ask yourself if you're willing to do what it takes to encounter God. Are you serious about it? Do you really believe that an encounter with God is possible, or is it just for other people to experience? Are you ready to re-engage in a passionate pursuit of God?

THE FINISH LINE

The undeniable truth is that we need thin places. If only for a moment, we need to be reminded that those wild, unpredictable encounters with God are real. And they are essential if we are to have an ongoing, relevant, and dangerous faith. We must pursue those moments when God interrupts our lives, those places where heaven and earth collide.

It isn't easy and it often flies in the face of common sense, but we must fight for these moments and ready ourselves for the experience when they come. We must be willing to do whatever it takes to get ourselves in position to encounter God in whatever way He chooses to show up. It's a struggle. Life is too short, the obstacles too big, the opposition too intense. Too many of us settle and abandon the journey at incredible costs to our souls. We need thin places. Often, we can't go on without them. That is what this book has been about.

As I've chronicled in these pages, I've come to points in my life where I wasn't sure I could go on spiritually. I wasn't sure this was real. I wasn't sure I would even buy what I was selling. I wasn't sure God was even hearing my prayers, let alone answering them, but that wasn't the hard part. The hard part was much worse.

The hard part was watching my kids battle through their journeys. At moments, my anger, frustration, and disappointments raged. I wasn't sure I would make it through. I wondered where God was and why He apparently wasn't with them in their darkest hours. Didn't he care what was happening to His kids? To my kids? The piercing question at that time was, "GOD, WHY ARE YOU SILENT?" I screamed that plea from my broken father's heart to my Father. And He was silent...

...until that moment on the boardwalk. That moment, that thin place changed everything.

But that question haunts me still. At times, it makes me question my spiritual journey to the core. Why does God so often seem so quiet? Why must there be extended times in the wilderness? Why couldn't Moses cross over to the promised land with the nation of Israel? Yes, he made a mistake, but seriously, after being God's chosen man to lead the people out of slavery, after decades of leading stubborn people and trying to obey God, why couldn't he experience this one thing that God had promised? Who wants to sign up for that kind of leadership journey? None of it makes sense.

Harbor Ministries was born out of my own struggles and questions. It was a hope that we could challenge and inspire leaders to keep pursuing God with all they've got. It was a belief that people could encounter the Creator in life-changing ways. It was a conviction that no matter what comes our way, no matter how intense the questions, the struggles, the doubts, no matter how long the time in the wilderness, no matter how deafening the silence, we can still see and experience God. It doesn't make sense, but I believe it. We believe it. There are these thin places where God disrupts our lives and reminds us that He has been here walking through all of it with us. All of it. The hell. The high water. The doubt. The rage. The apathy. All of it.

At the bottom of a midlife crash, struggling with failure, hopelessness, and a good dose of depression, I was ready to give up when I found myself on that mountain overlooking Quito, Ecuador, God interrupted my life, my pain, and my doubt. He showed me a course for a new kind of ministry to leaders centered on a belief that life-giving, life-altering encounters with God were not only possible, but probable.

Looking back, I still shake my head. The very first guy who showed up at the very first Harbor event looked at me and said, "My wife told me this was a cult and that I shouldn't come. I told her, 'I don't know who these people are, and this is something new, and I don't know really what this is about, but I'm so desperate to experience God that I have to go. I have to be reminded this is real. I need to encounter God. I can't go on as a pastor... I can't keep taking people to something I'm no longer able to experience myself. I have to go."

It made no sense, but he came and so did nineteen others who were desperate to encounter God as well. People who were ready to cast off the masks, the pretentions, the role-playing, and the posing. That's when it began to make sense.

Really, what Harbor does is create space and a rhythm to life that readies our souls to meet God in those thin places. I know that God brings those moments in unexpected and unpredictable ways, but over and over again I've realized that heaven and earth collide more often when we are ready, alert, and pursuing Him. And when He does bring us to a thin place, we understand in that moment how present God has been on the entire journey.

So it was when we finally reached the upper edge of that cliff in Iceland. Two dimensional black and white words on a flat page cannot contain the moment. It was a place of worship and awe. We were small and God was... more. Some fell to their knees, others were prostrate. Others went right up to the edge, seemingly ready to leap. And I stood beside my son. I urged him to keep taking his peers to places like this. I told him he has what it takes to lead others to be cliff chasers. He has what it takes to give people the hope, encouragement, and inspiration to keep moving, to keep asking questions, and to keep pursuing God.

Thin places are fuel for our journey. They give us a glimpse, however brief, into how life was meant to be all along.

So how about you? Are you ready to chase a cliff or two?

As the moments of writing this book come to a close, a few questions come to mind. How can we position ourselves to best be ready to experience those thin places? We talked about Exodus 3 when God meets Moses in a burning bush. Maybe God was there in the burning bush all along, but it was not until He saw Moses turn to the burning bush that He spoke. What we do know from this story is that it took action from both God and Moses. So what do we need to do to turn, to posture ourselves, toward God?

In *The Lord of the Rings: The Two Towers*, the second movie in the trilogy, Aragorn and Théoden, the king of Rohan, have a heated discussion. Evil was overtaking the land. Villages had been raided and people had been killed. The king felt his best move was to take his people to Helms Deep, a castle that had provided safety and refuge in the past. The king was in denial of the reality around him. In a powerful moment, Aragorn told the king, "War is upon you whether you believe it or not."

In our spiritual journeys, war is upon us, whether we acknowledge it or not. We are in a battle. Struggle, failure and disappointment will be with us throughout our lives. And if we're going to stay in the game as more than just players but as difference-makers, if we're going to be men and women who encourage, challenge, and inspire others at a time when this world desperately needs that, we need these thin places. We need the alertness to seek and find those moments when God interrupts our lives in tangible ways.

This world leaves us no choice. We need to wildly and relentlessly commit to a pursuit of God, no matter what life throws our way.

SPACE

Do you want to experience thin places? If you want to practice the themes of remembering, lightening your load, staying alert, and awakening your soul, one simple practice is crucial. It is an ancient practice, yet a discipline that has been largely ignored by the current Christian culture until recently. When we started dreaming about what a transformational experience would be like in Harbor Ministries, this became a central theme, the foundation to everything else we did. If there was one thing that has made a difference in my own life over the years it is this:

Space.

We must fight for regular times of space.

Webster defines space as, "a continuous area or expanse that is free, available or unoccupied." That definition works pretty well for what we are exploring here. In Harbor, we ask leaders to take a full day of quiet, a full day of space every month. We ask them to unplug, disconnect, enter this free, available, unoccupied space and listen.

Getting to a place where we can shut off the noise, do what it takes to settle ourselves down, then read, journal, and listen is a critical practice. It's a difference-making, life-changing practice. And the key word is practice. It will take the regular, committed practice of planning for and taking this extended time. You will struggle to take it. You will feel restless and guilty. It will take you a couple of hours to settle in. You will have to fight for it every time. But every time it will be worth it.

When you do get away, we have a simple tool to help focus your time: Look back and look forward. Ask yourself these questions:

• What has God been teaching me, showing me, and challenging me with over the last month?

• Are there any themes, passions, or burdens that have been present?

• Is there anything that has made me mad? Those times can give great insight.

Then look ahead:

• Is there anything I am burdened with, anxious about, or hoping for in the weeks ahead?

That's the simple roadmap I use. I take a journal, ask those questions, and many times the thoughts and words come. Other times I sit in extended times of quiet.

This of course is nothing new. We see this habit throughout the scriptures.

Moses took forty days to seek God. He stayed on that mountain until God spoke. And we know that several times, Jesus pulled away to the wilderness to be alone. He took forty days to strengthen himself and fight off the temptations that the enemy threw at him. Not until those forty days were finished was he truly ready for the task before him.

Throughout his three years of ministry, we often see Jesus pulling away to be alone. He pulled away after times of crisis. Soon after John the Baptist was killed we find Jesus alone in Matthew 14:13 (NASB). "Now when Jesus heard about John, He withdrew from there in a boat to a secluded place by Himself." He also sought solitude after times of success. Verses 22-23 say, "After He had sent the crowds away, He went up on the mountain by himself to pray." The people and the crowds following Him were increasing, and where do we find Jesus? Off in the wilderness spending time alone with God. Those who traveled with Jesus knew this practice of His, and He modeled it throughout the gospels.

So many current and former leaders considered this practice of solitude, and quiet—this practice of space—critical to their leadership journeys. Winston Churchill was notorious for a nightly swim and a quiet walk with his cigar. George Marshall referred to his weekly horse ride as sacred time. He was so committed to that time that his aides hesitated to interrupt him to tell him the news of the Pearl Harbor attack. My dad went fishing. Mark Batterson talks about going to the roof of the coffee house in downtown Washington, D.C. Eugene Peterson talks of his nightly walks in the woods. My friend Mike has to get his boat out on a lake to get that needed quiet and peace. Whenever I can, I get on my bike. It is a place of certain refuge. We need to have this time, this space to help balance the compression and pressure of leadership.

Fight for it. It is so worth it.

DANGER IN THE QUIET

I have always sought extended times of quiet. One of the themes of my life has been this longing for space—times to dream, listen, process, and shut off the noise. It started when I was young and would wander back to the pasture behind our house. I could spend hours thinking about the places I wanted to go and the things I wanted to do. There is often peace in this quiet, but I have learned not to seek the quiet for safety; for me, dangerous things often happen in the quiet.

Several winters ago, a major blizzard hit on Christmas Eve. For a few days, we were completely isolated. It took a major winter storm to force me into a needed change of pace. The quiet mornings gave me space to reflect on the previous months. It had been a rough year. I was at a point of transition, and had been through a season of fatigue, boredom, and restlessness.

In that forced, desperately needed quiet, God reminded me of the thin places where He had met me in the past, the unique and sometimes difficult ways He had broken through and revealed Himself to me.

If not for that space created by the blizzard, I would have been in real trouble.

The blizzard raged on, but in those cold, isolating winds I felt some renewal in my passion to pursue Him again. To meet Him in the quiet and solitude. To create space. Through the years, it has always been worth the fight to get these times alone with God. This time it just needed to be forced on me.

I believe the same is true for you. You can find renewal if you will create space, if you will practice seeking Him in extended times of quiet. But I'm hesitant to invite you to pursue God in this kind of space. It can be dangerous. You will be vulnerable. These extended times of solitude can be filled with minefields. In the last few years, these quiet times of listening have been a dangerous place for me. In the quiet, God has convicted me of things that should be changed, relationships I needed to let go of, and strongholds I needed to surrender. In the quiet I felt the nudge to leave a ministry I'd led for twenty years and step into an unsafe, uncertain new role. In the quiet I was led to start a new ministry using a counterintuitive strategy that could very easily fail.

But it does beg the question: What if you dare to turn off the distractions, unplug, and practice pursuing God in regular times of space? Might He meet you there? Get ready, because in the stillness and the quiet God will call you out. He will extend dangerous invitations to the kind of deep soul change that can lead to action. This just doesn't happen in a fifteen-minute quiet time with a to-do list and an agenda.

I recently read about a doctor who was tired and overworked. He spent long hours entrenched in treating multiple patients. He found himself ordering more and more tests, hoping that the tests would somehow produce the answers that his training, experience, and intuition should produce. Without rest, quiet, and the right amount of margin in his schedule, he had lost the ability to use his knowledge and skills as he needed to.

The same can be true for us. If we fail to create space, it can get very hard to hear and identify that still small voice we so desperately need. With no margin, that intuitive ability that others need from us can get dull or be lost completely. It happened in my journey, and if I had continued to follow the path I was on, a lot of things would have been at risk. You are at risk as well. We will get weary in the doing no matter how great the cause, and in our weariness, we may turn to everything else but the Source for direction and help. That is the place where another kind of danger can set in.

Psalm 91:1 (NASB) says, "He who dwells in the shelter of the Most High will abide in the shadow of the Almighty." I hope that you will find a way to create space—to rest, find refuge and hear clearly the whisper of God.

Elijah needed space and his journey may not be so different from ours. Let's look at his story in 1 Kings 19. Elijah had been through it. He sold out for God but it all seemed futile. The Philistine king killed the priests and vowed to pursue Elijah and kill him as well. Elijah was discouraged, disillusioned, and, in many ways, done. As we enter this story we find him in the heat of the day sitting under a small tree. There was not enough shade to break the crippling heat that burned him from the outside and the inside. Discouragement, disappointment, and likely some depression settled in. But there, away from the battle, away from the stress of defending God and demonstrating His power, there in that desperate place, Elijah began to hear God.

> Then he was told, 'Go stand on the mountain at attention before God. God will pass by. A hurricane wind ripped through the mountains, and shattered the rocks before God, but God wasn't found in the wind; after the wind an earthquake but God wasn't in the earthquake; and after the earthquake fire, but God wasn't in the fire, and after the fire a gentle and quiet whisper.
>
> 1 Kings 19:11-12 (TM)

The passage goes on to say that when Elijah heard the whisper, he covered his face with his cloak, and God spoke to him. I imagine that when he heard God's voice in that whisper, the healing, the rest, the strength, the sense that God was with him, returned.

Throughout history, people have sought space. I've been reading about

Irish monks who made a type of space their critical practice more than 1,600 years ago. They shared some things in common with the early Celtic Christians, including exile that ultimately expanded their reach. As I was reading Thomas Cahill's book, *How the Irish Saved Civilization*, I started a list.

Both groups were:

1. Committed to fighting for times of silence, solitude, extended times of worship, and listening.

2. Willing to go wherever and do whatever, and endure anything to make that happen.

3. Stoutheartedly willing to engage an enemy wherever and whenever.

4. Able to use solitude to strengthen themselves for critical missions. They knew solitude provides strength, courage, and resolve for the mission.

5. Exiled for the sake of the Gospel.

6. Unafraid of any obstacle that lay in wait.

7. Ready to take the mission beyond the safety and comfort of familiar places.

8. Were also committed to community.

9. Multiplied and expanded their reach by going out in teams.

Both groups undoubtedly understood the value of solitude, space, and silence. The Celtic Christians were some of the first to write about this idea of thin places. Moments they most likely first began to encounter after creating space. So, here is a practical invitation: Sometime in the next month, take a WHOLE day away. Shut off. Listen. If you don't schedule this time, it more than likely won't happen. Put it on your calendar now. Fight the resistance that tells you that you can't or won't or shouldn't.

A FEW THOUGHTS TO HELP:

- Go to a place where your spirit wakes up. Remember, location is everything! Find a place where distractions don't exist and where your phone can't ring, or leave the phone behind.
- Take a journal, a book, some music, whatever stirs you.
- To kick things off, read a favorite chapter in a book, listen to a favorite song.
- Then, just be quiet. Listen.

Take part of the day to reflect on your spiritual journey. Review the questions I've been asking you to consider in this book. Go back to a time or times when God uniquely revealed Himself to you. Where were you? Who were you with? What was going on in your life at the time? What did God say and how did you feel about Him speaking to you?

Then listen again.

Make this day of space the beginning of a journey that lasts a lifetime—a journey marked by the intentional pursuit of the still small voice, the gentle whisper that is the one we most need to hear.

Give yourself some grace. Space is counterintuitive in our culture that values busyness, achievement, production, and results. Creating space will take practice and time to develop a good rhythm. You must fight for this time. Our obnoxiously loud world will work against something as foreign as silence and space. You must carve it into your schedule and make it non-negotiable.

If you dare to develop this rhythm of creating space, you will become dangerous to the enemy. Dangerous vision, dangerous hope, dangerous steps of faith, dangerous contentment, and deep peace will be birthed in extended times of quiet and solitude. If you develop the regular practice of taking time to be alone and quiet before God, you will have a much better chance of living with rhythm and staying the course in your faith, at work, and with your family. You will be ready to step into whatever God has in store for you, and you will be much better equipped to finish well.

So, as you seek these times of space, I hope they will give you strength for the weeks, months, and years ahead. I hope that you will learn to trust your intuition, and, most importantly, to trust the still small voice of God.

PART FOUR

A RETURN TO THE CLIFF
AND THOSE THIN PLACES

THIN PLACES

Song by Harbor Accomplice Bryan Olesen

Wait

All I can do is wait

Will the silence ever break

The questions still remain unanswered

Why does a silent God want me to pray

Are these words just lost in space

Will anything really change if I cry out

I see the stars are lighting up the sky

Maybe You're telling me everything will be alright

Feels like heaven came down to earth tonight

For this moment

For this moment

My heart

A ship in a sea of storms

Just trying to keep true north

Trying to stay on course

Til it's over

Heaven came down to earth tonight

Feels like heaven came down to earth tonight

Feels like heaven came down to earth tonight

I believe it

I believe it

The stars are lighting up the sky

Maybe You're telling me everything will be alright

Feels like heaven came down to earth tonight

For this moment

For this moment

I see the stars are lighting up the sky

Maybe You're telling me everything will be alright

I don't to need to understand or know the reasons why

For this moment

For this moment

Download a free copy of this song at

www.thinplacesbook.com/song

A RETURN TO THE CLIFF

"I'm drawn to places that beguile and inspire, sedate and stir, places where for a few blissful moments I loosen my death grip on life, and can breathe again, it turns out these destinations have a name: thin places."

Eric Weiner, "Where Heaven and Earth Come Closer"

The New York Times

The band of Hobbits had just returned from their epic journey that had changed the fate of the world. They were gathered in a little pub back in the Shire. As they looked around, they realized that others had no sense of the incredible journey they had been on. They were unaware of the change that had taken place, of the destruction that had been averted because of the adventure and the bravery of these four hobbits. As they tipped their glasses in an unspoken toast, they knew this journey had connected them at a deep level. It had to feel like a lonely place, realizing that no one else would ever fully understand.

Sometimes the pursuit of thin places can feel like a moment in the Shire. It can be a very lonely place, a place others around you do not experience, and an idea few really connect with. It can be a place you will need to bravely pursue through many lonely moments. That moment in the Shire was shared by four soulmates bonded by an epic shared life experience. Sometimes life, and these pursuits of thin places, happen that way. But so many times it is a journey we make alone.

I took a day of space recently. I studied the last chapter in Moses' leadership journey. It's the part of his story that I have always struggled with. He has faithfully led stubborn people for forty years in the wilderness. He has stayed true to God through all of it. He had his mistakes, and at one point disobeys God. The consequence: he will not pass into the Promised Land with the people.

God takes Moses up the mountain to look at the Promised Land. This is the moment for the nation of Israel, this is the promise of God that was passed on through generations of slavery. This is what God called Moses to do! But Moses will not live to see the fulfillment of the promise. It doesn't seem fair, or even right. It doesn't make any sense.

God said to Moses, 'Climb up into the Abarim Mountains and look over at the land that I am giving to the People of Israel. When you've had a good look you'll be joined to your ancestors in the grave—yes, you also along with Aaron your brother. This goes back to the day when the congregation quarreled in the Wilderness of Zin and you didn't honor me in holy reverence before them in the matter of the waters, the Waters of Meribah (Quarreling) at Kadesh in the Wilderness of Zin.'

Moses responded to God: 'Let God, the God of the spirits of everyone living, set a man over this community to lead them, to show the way ahead and bring them back home so God's community will not be like sheep without a shepherd.'

Numbers 27:12-17 (TM)

But as you read this passage, and as I thought through again, it struck me that it did not seem to matter to Moses. Even though this moment seems intensely lonely after a forty-year quest, the Promised Land was not the end game. Being in God's presence was the end game. As Moses walked up that mountain, he knew the struggle would soon be over and that he would be in the presence of God all the time, not just in the thin places this side of heaven.

A certain peace has overcome me, a peace that says God must have been enough in that moment. Moses seemed at peace. In this passage, you don't see or hear struggle. There is not a report of complaint or resistance. It's not hard to imagine that God took Moses up that mountain as a reminder of all the thin places where they had met before, many times on other mountain tops. Maybe God wanted to reassure Moses that he would be okay; that the coming transition might be scary but God would be with him through all of it. And I wonder if he took him up that mountain to give him a glimpse of the Promised Land and let him see the people moving toward that promise. And just maybe God whispered to him, "Moses, well done. No one else will really understand what you have gone through in leading these people, but I do. And because you listened, because you were faithful, because you trusted me... this moment happened for them." That perspective changes the story for me.

What happens next? I like to think that Moses comes to this realization that God is enough, that even the crossing into the Promised Land pales in comparison to being in God's presence. Even as he walked up that mountain, God was coming alongside that next generation of leaders. In a personal, relational conversation, much like he had with Moses, God made a promise to the new leader, Joshua.

After the death of Moses, the servant of God, God spoke to Joshua, Moses' assistant:

'Moses my servant is dead. Get going. Cross this Jordan River, you and all the people. Cross to the country I'm giving to the People of Israel. I'm giving you every square inch of the land you set your foot on—just as I promised Moses. From the wilderness and this Lebanon east to the Great River, the Euphrates River—all the Hittite country— and then west to the Great Sea. It's all yours. All your life, no one will be able to hold out against you. In the same way I was with Moses, I'll be with you. I won't give up on you; I won't leave you. Strength! Courage! You are going to lead this people to inherit the land that I promised to give their ancestors. Give it everything you have, heart and soul. Make sure you carry out The Revelation that Moses commanded you, every bit of it. Don't get off track, either left or right, so as to make sure you get to where you're going. And don't for a minute let this Book of The Revelation be out of mind. Ponder and meditate on it day and night, making sure you practice everything written in it. Then you'll get where you're going; then you'll succeed. Haven't I commanded you? Strength!

Courage! Don't be timid; don't get discouraged. God, your God, is with

you every step you take.'"

Joshua 1:1-9 (TM)

The last moments in Moses' leadership journey were critical. As I have processed the many times in my own journey when I have been at that desperate place—that moment of decision, that moment at the crossroad—experience has told me that is not a bad place to be. In fact, it can be a pretty good place to be. In those moments, I have been willing to risk, to go anywhere, to encounter anything just to get myself in a place to truly encounter God.

My spiritual journey had become a series of dos and don'ts. It had become a disconnected, disjointed journey. My head, heart, and emotions were in very different places. I needed to see, hear, and experience God in a different way. The wander started to come the first time I read the book *Wild at Heart.* Finally, someone who was not afraid to ask the questions my friends and I were asking. Finally, someone who was willing to break through the spiritual taboos... the lists of shoulds and should nots, duties, and obligations. Finally, someone who could name the struggles and call out a faith that had become void of risk and any sense of adventure. That started my journey. I learned that if I would relentlessly seek God, He could be found. That if I was willing to desperately pursue new spaces and places, that if I was willing to return to some of the places God had shown up in my past, there was hope that life could be different.

And one of those thin places of hope for me and this band of seven that journeyed to Iceland was this crazy cliff we were chasing. It represented so much for all of us, and the moment we arrived there did not disappoint.

But as I left that incredible place, I felt myself struggling. It is so much like life; you take the highs and lows, the victories and the defeats; sometimes things make perfect sense, and at other times everything seems to unravel. Sometimes God seems close, and in the next moment so distant.

So, it was with me as we left the cliff. As I returned from Iceland there was emotion that I did not expect. There was deep inspiration, which I did expect, but there was also deep sadness that was hard for me to explain. This is some of what I wrote in my journal on the plane ride home.

Journal Entry, Aug 5, 2016

Deeply inspired, yet Deeply sad.

Deeply inspired...

   -by His creation

   -by His wildness

   -by the raw, risky, awe-inspiring encounters with His creation

   -by His sheer abundance... it had to be part of what early creation
   was like

   -to take the next steps

   -to keep encouraging others to take steps toward the cliff

   -to help others not lose sight of needed cliff moments

But I am also deeply saddened on this ride home that...

   -at least for now, the quest is over

   -we only get a glimpse

   -I could have done more to help create even better moments
   at the finish of this epic trip

-I could have said more, done more to help others experience this

  even more deeply

-I won't always have this kind of connection

-We will never pass this exact same way again

This must be what it feels like when you have pursued, chased, hoped for, and finally accomplished something, then asked, 'What now?' I feel sad like a climber who has reached the summit and wonders what's next. That climber has a sense that he can't stay there, he can't live there... and a deep sense that he will not be able to return there in the same way ever again.

So, Why so sad?

  - that it feels like there may not be another "first" discovery moment of the cliff again... not like this.

  -that I can't sustain the wonder, the hope, the anticipation that the cliff represents

  -for others who seem unable to see it... who just can't seem to see and experience these moments.

  -for others who are drifting away from this pursuit...for them and for myself, who so often can't see through the fog and pain to find Him in the thin places that may appear

  -for the church that is missing it...missing the truth that God is adventurous, wild, sometimes unpredictable, raw, untamed, and mysterious

  -sad that there seems to be so few frontiers... so few new

discoveries... so few places like Iceland left.

Yet, I feel deeply determined

-to keep chasing cliffs no matter how crazy it seems to me or to others

- to not let the enemy steal, kill, or destroy what I have discovered here

-to keep inviting others to chase those cliffs as well

-to keep inviting, inspiring, and challenging others to get themselves in spaces where they can see and experiences thin places.

The truth is we need thin places. Our souls and our lives ache for them More than that, recognizing, embracing, and responding to the thin places when they come is central to a relevant and impactful faith that we and this world are desperate for. We must pursue those moments when God interrupts our lives, those places where heaven and earth collide. We must be willing to do whatever it takes to get ourselves in position to encounter God in whatever way He shows up. Life is too short, the obstacles too big, the opposition too intense. Too many of us abandon the spiritual journey at incredible costs to our souls. That's why we need these thin places. We need to keep chasing cliffs. I am convinced that no matter how hard the moments, or how intense the questions, the struggle, or doubt, no matter how long the time in the wilderness, no matter how deafening the silence, there are still spaces and places where we can see and experience God.

I said this earlier and I believe it's worth mentioning again: In our spiritual journeys, war is upon us whether we acknowledge it or not. Struggle, loneliness, obstacles, loss, and disappointment will be with us throughout our lives. But if we're going to be leaders who challenge and inspire others, we need thin places. We simply must do what it takes to ready ourselves for those moments when God interrupts our lives—those moments of awe, wonder, challenge, and invitation.

The world needs cliff chasers, passionate and relentless dreamers; men and women willing to put it all on the line, ready to recognize, step into, and embrace the thin places whenever and however they come.

God, help us in this space, in this moment and the moments to come, to wildly and relentlessly pursue you.

PART FIVE
AFTERWARD

AFTERWARD

As I was completing this manuscript I found myself back in that place of questioning and doubt. I continued to be in the middle of what became some of the toughest months of my life. This last year has been a journey of extremes—times of seeing God show up like never before, yet times of dream-crushing disappointments and pain with those close to me.

So many hard, tragic, exciting, and unsettling events have occurred around the world in 2017. But strangely, one that has really impacted me deeply is the passing of Tom Petty. Through the years, music has been a powerful, centering, and deeply impacting form of art for me. It has been an avenue for marking key moments and remembering significant times. So often, it has just plain been fun! Music has provided a needed refuge, an occasional escape, and offered me some hope and peace at critical times.

I have loved Petty's music since college. The lyrics and movement of his music have come to represent so many of the seasons, thoughts, highs, lows, and journey of my own life. I saw Petty live in concert several times over the years and he never disappointed. He was not a poser, was never political on stage, he did not say too much, he just let the power of the music speak for itself. He always seemed thankful and showed a deep appreciation to his fans. Like so many other great artists and performers before him, he came from a deeply painful past. But the pain, struggles, and some of his choices at the end did not change or diminish the impact of his work. Despite his wild success and some of the ongoing struggles in his life, he retained this genuine and humble stage presence that was always evident through the years.

In my experience, Petty's performances became more authentic, powerful and impacting in his later years. He seemed to enjoy performing more and was fully in the moment the last few times I saw him.

There were many memorable concerts, like his show at Red Rocks Amphitheatre in Denver a few years ago. It was there I remember him talking about his band mates and how much they still enjoyed touring together. At that point, much of the band had toured together for more than thirty years, and Petty said they enjoyed the music and the tours more as they got older. They seemed to be fully engaged—not just performing, but committed to really living in the moments they were given.

As good as they were through the years, they were clearly at their best on their 40th Anniversary Tour in the summer of 2017. It was so incredible, I saw him twice over the summer. The first experience was in June, in Iowa with my son and two good friends. As the concert started, it was clear something special was about to happen. One of the friends with me, a musician himself, remarked on how powerful the music was in that moment. For three hours, people were absorbed in the experience with Tom Petty and the Heartbreakers. I have been to a lot of concerts, and have been a spectator at a lot of great sporting events. I have seen my favorite team win championships in person three times. But I have never experienced thousands of people being so totally in the moment as they were that night, fully engaged, soaking it all in, having fun, letting go of the struggles and things that were weighing them down. That night the music became much bigger than Petty himself, and he knew it. It was awesome, and my younger son became an instant fan.

I got to see Petty again a couple of months later at the end of his tour, in Del Mar Beach north of San Diego. As it turned out, this was one of the last concerts he would ever do.

In the middle of the mess our family was walking through, I found myself in San Diego for a Harbor Ministry event. I almost didn't go because things were so intense back home, but God clearly had me there for many reasons. The impact of that Rhythm in Twenty event went deep, and the time with the young leaders who had gathered from around the country was rich. Yet, in my own journey, I was hurting, and found myself again questioning God and my faith in big ways. Throughout the previous months, I had seen time and time again, that no matter how hard things were for me personally, no matter how difficult the faith journey, or how deep the questioning, God was on the move.

Strength started to return as I sat for hours by the water near the San Diego Harbor. I spent hours thinking back over the intense pain, trying to make some sense of it. But mostly I was just quiet. It had been one of the most difficult yet impacting seasons of my life, and now I was back at this harbor, back at this place that had meant so much to me over the years. I felt like I was on a spiritual pilgrimage. That specific spot in San Diego has been holy ground for me. Sometimes we need to return to those holy places, those thin places where we've encountered God in the past, places where He again might interrupt our lives and stories.

As I leaned into the extended time of quiet, inspiration to write and journal crept back for the first time in months. Hope trickled in. Petty was playing north of San Diego that Sunday night, but I was undecided if I should stay an extra day or head home. I ended up staying and was given a ticket to the outdoor concert. As we stood on the sand as the sun set, Petty and the Heartbreakers took the stage, and I quickly realized that night was a God kind of gift. Even as intense storms raged in my life, heaven and earth collided in a thin place that I desperately needed. As it turned out, I was not the only one dealing with pain that night. It was revealed later that Petty had performed much of the summer with a broken hip. That constant physical struggle, and perhaps some ache in his soul as well, lead him to address the pain in some difficult ways. But despite the pain, he endured. He still brought his best that night, and he finished the tour that he was so passionate about.

That night, more than any in recent memory, I was able to drop the burdens I'd been shouldering for a few hours just to be in the moment. I felt like a kid again, surrounded by the power of music; a power that reminds us of hope, brings healing and clarity, and simply immerses us in joyous celebration.

The concert represented so much for me. It became a place of deep connection to the music and to those I was with. There was also this connection to so many people I had never met before, and with it, a sense that we may not ever have this kind of moment again. Honestly, as I listened to comments Petty himself was making, I believe he also had a sense he may not walk this path again, that time was short. We were truly in a thin place.

Concerts have become markers for me. I Kings 8:56-58 has been a rallying cry for the leadership events we do. "Blessed be God who has given peace to His people Israel, just as He said He would do. May God, our very own God, continue to be with us, just as He was with our ancestors—may He never give up and walk out on us. May He keep us centered and devoted to Him, following the life path He has cleared. Watching the signposts, walking at the pace and rhythms He laid down for our ancestors." (TM)

These concerts that surrounded such heartbreak, struggle, and disruption in my life became significant signposts that have helped me continue this journey. The reminders came in Petty's lyrics as I listened to his music throughout the summer. Whether to remind me to keep "Runnin' Down a Dream," no matter what life throws at me, or recall how important it is that I'm "Learning to Fly" and continuing to learn and press forward. More than ever I know I need to take a higher view of the struggles and obstacles that get thrown in front of me. Throughout the summer, I began to realize at an even deeper level that I need this higher view, this different perspective, to see a way through. And even though coming down from these high places is the hardest part, I must fight for those moments, and find consistent ways to get above my struggles.

Petty's music helped me to "keep swinging," to keep chasing the things I am called to and am most passionate about. The concerts became a great challenge for me. No matter how old he was, Tom Petty kept bringing it. He kept exercising his passion and using his talent to the very end. He did, in fact, go down swinging.

For sure these concerts became a powerful reminder and challenge to not back down, and to stand my ground. None of us can afford to back down. Life is just too short.

In Petty's words:

Well, I won't back down

No, I won't back down

You can stand me up to the gates of Hell

But I won't back down.

Well I know what's right

I got just one life

In a world that's keeps pushin' me around

But I'll stand my ground

And I won't back down.

"I Won't Back Down" by Jeff Lynne and Tom Petty

Sometimes we want to box God in. We often think truth can only come from the Bible or through some pre-defined church-like experiences. That is just not true. Our creative God made all of this; music, nature, writing, art, and the spoken word. He has hidden His characteristics and a sense of who He is in creation and in other people and the art they create. We just need to pause, look, listen, and wait to see it. Somehow God spoke to me time and time again through the brilliant creative talent of Tom Petty.

As crazy as it sounds, these two nights changed me in ways that are hard to describe. They were moments that God used to give me a glimpse into who He is, moments that were both fun and deep, wild and inspiring. They were thin place moments that I will never forget.

Don't back down. Keep swinging. Keep pursuing the Wild Goose.

Keep chasing cliffs.

SHARE YOUR STORY

Now that you've heard my story of thin place moments, I want to hear yours. If you've encountered God in moments of unexpected clarity and grace that have disrupted your life, would you be willing to share that experience with me and with others?

We're creating a Thin Place Community where we can inspire and challenge one another to keep chasing cliffs and seeking encounters with the Wild Goose.

To share your own thin place story with this community, please call the number below and leave us a voice mail. We can't wait to hear your story!

Onward,

Tim

Call this number to leave your thin place story:

877-232-5057

RESOURCES AND REFERENCES

The following books, music and movies have shaped my thinking about thin places, leadership, and our own wild hearts. I encourage you to read, listen to, and watch.

PREFACE

Barton, Ruth Haley. *Strengthening the Soul of Your Leadership*. Downers Grove, IL: InterVarsity Press, 2008.

Batterson, Mark. *Wild Goose Chase*. New York: Doubleday, 2008.

Cahill, Thomas. *How the Irish Saved Civilization*. New York: Anchor, 1996.

Eldredge, John. *Wild at Heart*. Nashville: Thomas Nelson, 2001.

THE CALL OF THIN PLACES

Sigur Rós. "Glósóli." Takk…, Track 2. EMI Records. 2010.

Batterson, Mark. Wild Goose Chase.

THE PERFECT STORM

Barton, Ruth Haley. *Strengthening the Soul of Your Leadership*. Page 97.

BOREDOM

The Breakfast Club. Directed by John Hughes. Los Angeles: Universal Pictures, 1985.

FATIGUE

McKnight, Scott. "Burnout for Pastors." Jesus Creed. Beliefnet. http://www.beliefnet.com/columnists/jesuscreed/2007/08/burnout-for-pastors.html

Krejcir, Dr. Richard. "Statistics on Pastors: 2016 Update."

Churchleadership.org. http://www.churchleadership.org/apps/articles/

default.asp?blogid=4545&view=post&articleid=Statistics-on-Pastors-

2016-Update&link=1&fldKeywords=&fldAuthor=&fldTopic=0

Jayson, Sharon. "Who's Feeling Stressed? Young Adults, New Survey Shows."

USA Today, Feb. 7, 2013.

REMEMBER

Peterson, Eugene. *The Message: Solo-An Uncommon Devotional.*

Colorado Springs, CO: NavPress, 2007. Introduction.

LIGHTEN

The Secret Life of Walter Mitty. Directed by Ben Stiller. Los Angeles: 20th

Century Fox, 2013.

The Book of Eli. Directed by Albert Hughes and Allen Hughes. Los Angeles:

Columbia Pictures, 2010.

ALERT

Junip. "Don't Let It Pass." Fields, Track 8. Mute Records. 2010.

Barton, Ruth Haley. *Strengthening the Soul of Your Leadership.*

AWAKEN

Mumford and Sons. "Awake My Soul." Sigh No More, Track 10.

Glassnote Records. 2010.

The Perfect Storm. Directed by Wolfgang Petersen. Los Angeles:

Warner Bros., 2000.

Chasing Mavericks. Directed by Michael Apted and Curtis Hanson.

Los Angles: Fox 2000 Pictures, 2012.

Eldrege, John. *Beautiful Outlaw.* Nashville, TN. Faithwords, 2013.

THE ARRIVAL

Ahronson, Dr. Kristján. "Irish and Scots may have been first to settle Iceland, researcher finds." Medievalists.net.

The Lord of the Rings: The Two Towers. Directed by Peter Jackson. Los Angeles: New Line Cinema, 2010.

A RETURN TO THE CLIFF

Bryan Olesen. "Thin Places." Mydeas Music. MusicMissions.org. Download the song at www.thinplacesbook.com/song

Weiner, Ed. "Where Heaven and Earth Come Closer." The New York Times, March 9, 2012.

AFTERWARD

Tom Petty. "I Won't Back Down." Full Moon Fever, Track 10. MCA Records. 1989.

ABOUT THE AUTHOR

Tim Bohlke is the founder of Harbor Ministries, a journey that encourages, challenges and inspires leaders to live with rhythm, leave a legacy and finish well.

Tim has experienced the challenging and sometimes rough seas of leadership in his roles as an executive leader, pastor, teacher, coach, and counselor. He is passionate about being a husband and dad, and has been married to Marcia for more than thirty years. Tim and Marcia have three grown children and make their home in Lincoln, Nebraska. Tim loves traveling, biking, the mountains around Crested Butte, the San Diego boardwalk, and creating meaningful experiences for his family and others.

Tim plans to continue chasing cliffs and seeking ways to disrupt the status-quo leadership story.

Learn more about Tim's work at harborministries.com

Made in the USA
Columbia, SC
13 May 2018